Y0-DBK-955

WITHDRAWN

COMPETING VISIONS
THE NONPROFIT SECTOR IN THE TWENTY-FIRST CENTURY

Alan J. Abramson
Director, Nonprofit Sector Research Fund, The Aspen Institute
Editor, Nonprofit Sector Research Fund Dialogue Series

PERSPECTIVES FROM A CONFERENCE CONVENED BY THE NONPROFIT SECTOR RESEARCH FUND • JULY 1995

Nonprofit Sector Research Fund Dialogue Series
The Aspen Institute

HIEBERT LIBRARY
FRESNO PACIFIC UNIV.-M. B. SEMINARY
FRESNO, CA 93702

For additional copies of this publication, please contact:

Nonprofit Sector Research Fund
The Aspen Institute
1333 New Hampshire Ave., NW, Suite 1070
Washington, DC 20036
Phone: (202) 736-5800 • **Fax:** (202) 467-0790
E-mail: nsrf@aspeninst.org
Website: http://www.aspeninst.org/dir/polpro/nsrf/nsrf1.html

Copyright © 1997 by The Aspen Institute

The Aspen Institute
Suite 1070
1333 New Hampshire Avenue, N.W.
Washington, DC 20036

Published in the United States of America in 1997
by The Aspen Institute

All rights reserved

Printed in the United States of America

ISBN: 0-89843-211-1

Editorial Support for
Competing Visions: The Nonprofit Sector in the Twenty-First Century
by Spann Publications Consulting, Pittsburgh, PA

The Aspen Institute

Nonprofit Sector Research Fund

Mission Statement

Through grantmaking for research and dissemination, the Nonprofit Sector Research Fund seeks to expand knowledge of nonprofit activities, impacts, and values and promotes the use of new knowledge to improve nonprofit practices and inform public policy. The Fund also seeks to enhance nonprofit research by increasing the legitimacy and visibility of nonprofit scholarship; encouraging new investment in sector research; supporting the exploration of tough, neglected questions; and enlarging the number of creative scholars and practitioners interested in pursuing nonprofit studies.

Publications

The Nonprofit Sector Research Fund produces several publications, including grant guidelines; an annual report; working papers which present findings of Fund-supported research; *Nonprofit Research News*, a newsletter reporting on the Fund's activities and grants; the *Nonprofit Research Forum*, a periodical that features researcher and practitioner conversations about new Fund-sponsored research; the *Practitioner Viewpoint Series*, which draws on the leadership experience of nonprofit professionals; and the *Nonprofit Sector Research Fund Dialogue Series*, which offers perspectives from the Fund's conferences.

Funders

Bertelsmann Science Foundation
Carnegie Corporation of New York
The Ford Foundation
Frey Foundation
The Wallace Alexander Gerbode Foundation
The Walter and Elise Haas Fund
The William Randolph Hearst Foundation
The James Irvine Foundation

The W.K. Kellogg Foundation
The Lilly Endowment, Inc.
McGregor Fund
The Andrew W. Mellon Foundation
The Charles Stewart Mott Foundation
The David and Lucile Packard Foundation
The Rockefeller Brothers Fund
and others

Nonprofit Sector Research Fund Council

Virginia A. Hodgkinson, Co-Chair
Research Professor of Public Policy, Georgetown University

Russy D. Sumariwalla, Co-Chair
President and CEO Emeritus, United Way International

Carol L. Barbeito
President, Applied Research and Development Institute

Elizabeth T. Boris
Director, Center on Nonprofits and Philanthropy, The Urban Institute

Dennis A. Collins
President, The James Irvine Foundation

Gary Delgado
Executive Director, Applied Research Center

Pablo S. Eisenberg
President, Center for Community Change

Christopher J. Makins (ex officio)
Executive Vice President, The Aspen Institute

Terry T. Saario

Hildy Simmons
Managing Director, J.P. Morgan and Company, Inc.

John G. Simon
Professor of Law, Yale University

Julian Wolpert
Professor of Geography, Public Affairs, and Urban Planning, Princeton University

Staff
Alan J. Abramson, Director
Cinthia H. Schuman, Associate Director
David Williams, Program Coordinator
Susan D. Krutt, Program Assistant
Britton A. Walker, Administrative Assistant

Table of Contents

Preface

We are happy to present the first volume in the new *Nonprofit Sector Research Fund Dialogue Series*. The series is designed to provide perspectives from Fund conferences as well as the full text of papers used to spark conference debate and dialogue.

Competing Visions: The Nonprofit Sector in the Twenty-First Century struck us as an appropriate series starting point because its provocative papers ask us to consider anew three of the most fundamental questions that can be asked of the nonprofit sector:

- What are its unique and enduring roles in society?
- What are its most significant challenges as the new century approaches?
- What new directions should it consider taking?

The answers that our authors provide to these questions are intelligent and passionate. Like most answers to questions of basic identity, however, they are debatable and sometimes controversial. Yet we believe they offer nourishing food for thought.

The following introduction provides a brief summary of the themes that emerged from the papers as a group. After this introduction, readers will find the papers themselves. We hope this arrangement will suit both those who want to scan for major ideas only and those who want to read for details.

We are happy to have provided the forum for this vitally important discussion, and we look forward to continuing the dialogue initiated at the conference by funding new research on the role and prospects of the nonprofit sector as it confronts emerging challenges.

It is a pleasure to have an additional venue—the *Nonprofit Sector Research Fund Dialogue Series*—through which to disseminate research findings to policy makers, nonprofit practitioners, scholars, and other citizens whose combined efforts will determine the future of the sector.

I would like to gratefully acknowledge the support of our funders and the contributions of conference participants, Fund staff and Council, and the staff at Spann Publications Consulting in producing this volume. The views expressed in the following essays are the authors' and do not necessarily represent those of the Nonprofit Sector Research Fund or The Aspen Institute.

We invite readers to continue the conversations begun at our conferences by sending us their comments on this and other Fund publications.

Alan J. Abramson
Director
Nonprofit Sector Research Fund
The Aspen Institute

Introduction

This era of massive transition brings to mind an ancient and arresting Chinese curse: "May you live in interesting times." The business sector continues a major restructuring effort characterized by new ways of defining its mission, customers, products and workforce. Government, too, is "reinventing" itself—most obviously through a process of devolution that is reordering relationships between federal, state, and local government. Tight budgets are the order of the day, and major entitlement programs, notably Aid to Families with Dependent Children (AFDC), are being replaced with block grant funding that is reconstructing government's compact with the less fortunate and dramatically altering human service systems throughout the country.

The nonprofit sector, so much a part of these systems and the fabric of American society, is also registering the stresses of transition. The old consensus about its proper role shows signs of breaking down, and it is only natural—in view of the reforms afoot in other sectors—that it, too, should be reimagining its future. *Competing Visions: The Nonprofit Sector in the Twenty-first Century* contributes to the rethinking process necessary to produce a new consensus. The ten papers collected here were presented at the Nonprofit Sector Research Fund's 1995 conference. Taken together, they provide a set of provocative, lively, and quite different perspectives on the sector's role, its major challenges, and possible future directions.

In spite of the many different views held by the nine authors, readers will see that there is general agreement on the importance of a strong nonprofit sector capable of providing key human services, paying special attention to the less fortunate in society, strengthening community and democracy, and serving as a vehicle for the expression of charitable impulses.

At the same time, however, many of the authors express concern about the current and future capacity of the sector to carry out these important functions. Doubters defined a number of bracing challenges: more visible and contentious class and race divisions, less political and financial support for the sector, and more service demands as society becomes more sharply divided into those who have and those who need.

How should the sector respond to these challenges? And what are the implications of the sector's actions? As the papers seek to answer these questions, they sketch the broad outlines of several possible new directions for the sector in the 21st century and clearly identify additional research needed to inform sector policy and practice.

Nurturing Democratic Values and Community

In her essay, "Thoughts About the Nonprofit Sector: Now and Into the 21st Century," Sara Meléndez focuses on potential major new declines in government support of nonprofits, and she proposes steps nonprofits can take to prepare for this challenge. She reminds us of the sector's power to unify and of its rich history of serving as the voice of society's under-represented or unheard groups. Meléndez urges the sector to be more effective in publicizing its strengths and defending its role in society if it is to withstand this period of government retrenchment.

Jean Bethke Elshtain echoes the concerns raised by Meléndez and more specifically details America's fall into a "spiral of delegitimation," reflecting the erosion of traditional democratic ideas, civic engagement, and trust in institutions in recent years. Citing the historically prominent role of small scale civic associations in fostering democratic values and community participation, Elshtain believes nonprofits can play a crucial role in maintaining open, democratic dialogue, enhancing civic action, and rebuilding civil society.

This model of the nonprofit as catalyst for positive change is shared by Michael Miller, who explains how community-based, grassroots organizations can act as effective agents of change in renewing the fabric of communities. Such groups can encourage disadvantaged or marginalized individuals to assume important roles in their communities and fight for their rights in local decision-making forums. From Miller's perspective, many nonprofits seem well-equipped to reinforce democratic values and promote civic participation among those groups which are likely to feel the most alienated by the political processes of the late twentieth century.

In proposing this role for nonprofits, Miller suggests that if citizens are to engage in positive change, it is vital that they be able to see a connection between their actions and what happens in the world.

William Schambra picks up this theme by presenting a few vignettes of deeply committed people strengthening their communities. The individuals Schambra introduces believe that they can make a difference, and they are having significant impact in their spheres of influence. Yet according to Schambra, traditional, large scale, top-down systems of service delivery can ignore the capacity of the disadvantaged to do for themselves through a network of grassroots nonprofit initiatives. He raises the issue of bias in the sector against clients: this bias can have classist and racial overtones, though it is often disguised by helping gestures. Schambra believes that the sector's brightest hope for the future can be found in community-based nonprofits that value and use their clients' motivation and first-hand knowledge of local needs. Here, he says, is where the nonprofit and philanthropic communities should focus their energies.

Commercialization: A Double-Edged Sword

According to several conference participants, rising commercialization within the sector brings hope and danger in equal measures: as the sector experiments with commercialization, it increases access to resources, but risks compromising its mission and tax exempt status. Edward Skloot and tax specialist Janne Gallagher evaluate the costs and benefits of heightened commercial activity by nonprofits.

As fee-for-service operations become more prevalent, the distinction between nonprofits and for-profits is blurred. As a result, nonprofits are increasingly called upon to justify exactly what qualifies their work as "charitable" and entitles them to tax exemption. Gallagher and Skloot argue that nonprofits cannot afford to lose sight of the charitable aspects of their missions if they hope to retain special tax status, and perhaps more importantly, reinforce social trust in their work. They must also diversify their income sources in this era of government retrenchment and flat charitable giving.

Avoiding Government's "Fatal Embrace"

Questions about the tax-exempt status of nonprofits raise the thorny subject of the relationship between government and the nonprofit sector. Douglas Besharov and Peter Goldberg explore this changing relationship by looking at the impact of government cutbacks and the devolution of power to state and local governments. Both Besharov and Goldberg examine the paradoxical nature of government support: on the one hand, human and social service agencies have been heavily dependent on federal dollars for roughly one-third of their budgets; however, the top-down nature of public funding, coupled with regulations placed on these funds, may limit the flexibility of nonprofits and cause charitable organizations to stray from their missions. Goldberg and Besharov point to the possibility of Congress enacting the Istook-McIntosh Amendment as a case-in-point. This legislation would bar any tax-exempt organization receiving federal funds from using more than 5 percent of its total budget for advocacy activities.

Besharov suggests that nonprofits lessen their dependence on direct public funding and thereby avoid "government's fatal embrace." He objects to government's current method of picking "winners and losers" through its allocation of funds among service providers. He believes that recipients of services can, in most cases, make more informed decisions about who should serve their needs than government can. Besharov recommends that current funding policies be replaced with a bottom-up form of "reimbursed co-payment system," in which consumers, or clients, partially pay for services rendered and government reimburses nonprofits for the balance.

The challenge of providing quality services while relying on government funds is also cause for concern for Goldberg. Although budget cuts will place immediate financial pressure on nonprofits, he warns agencies against being passive bystanders to this process. He urges the sector to involve itself actively in the public debate around devolution issues because policy makers have little awareness of, and thus give scarce consideration to, the value of publicly-funded nonprofit services.

Creating Jobs in an Era of Retrenchment

Jeremy Rifkin's vision of the future role of the nonprofit sector hinges on the changing relationships between the independent sector, the public, and the government. He focuses on the effects of the information revolution on the global economy, warning that technological advances will wipe out entire categories of manufacturing and service industry jobs. He points to the inability of government and most industries to prepare for this global displacement of labor, and argues that the nonprofit sector is a prime area for potential job creation.

Rifkin also explores the usefulness of providing tax credits or deductions for people who donate their time to volunteer efforts. This kind of initiative might be an incentive to participate for millions of Americans whose time and financial resources are increasingly limited, he says. In both of his essays, Rifkin stresses the role of nonprofits as the cohesive, community-based force that can hold the diverse interests of America together.

Directions for the Future

In any conversation in which diverse ideas are presented and explored, specific questions emerge and demand further attention. At this conference, participants urged further research to answer questions that fall into two distinct groups: questions that deal with civic engagement and questions that deal with funding and commercialization.

- What is the contribution of community organizations to the formation of "social capital," the bonds among citizens that facilitate collective action? What are the indications that citizens are—or are not—disengaging from communities?
- What are the advantages and disadvantages of increasing the sector's reliance on grassroots, sometimes religiously-oriented organizations to re-engage citizens and deliver needed services?
- What are the advantages and disadvantages for government, nonprofits, and other interests in direct (e.g., grants, contracts) versus indirect (e.g., vouchers, copayments) government support of nonprofits?
- What are the benefits and costs of providing special subsidies, such as income, property, and sales tax exemptions, to nonprofit organizations?
- How dependent are nonprofits on commercial income, and what is the impact of such reliance on the operation of nonprofits?
- What are the likely impacts of instituting new, more stringent tests for tax-exempt status?
- Are the boundaries between the public, nonprofit, and for-profit sectors blurring, and if so, what are the consequences?

While there were diverse views among conference participants about the particular options that should be pursued by the nonprofit sector, some strategies emerged from the discussion as being worth the sector's serious consideration and perhaps implementation:

- encourage nonprofit activity at the grassroots level to tap the energy of ordinary citizens and reinvigorate communities;
- secure the financial and human resources of nonprofits, perhaps through new mechanisms such as a tax credit for volunteering;
- explore the shift of government support of the sector from direct contracts to indirect government assistance that goes to clients who then choose where to purchase services;
- consider linking tax-exempt status and other subsidies to the requirement that nonprofits derive a portion of their revenues from charitable giving; and
- increase public awareness of the nonprofit sector to facilitate policy making on sector issues.

The ways in which the sector takes up its challenges and possibilities will define its identity and mission in years to come. These papers should provoke further conversation and provide sector leaders and researchers with valuable food for thought.

Thoughts About the Nonprofit Sector: Now and Into the 21st Century

Sara E. Meléndez

King Solomon said that there is nothing new under the sun. In some ways, that is certainly true about the independent sector. There are recurring themes and issues that appear with regularity, varying degrees of intensity, and with new wrinkles, such as the erosion of trust caused by reports of wrongdoing and attacks on the sector's tax-exempt status and on its right to advocate and lobby. Other issues are always with us, like the issue of inadequate resources. But Solomon could not know about technology and how it would change our lives, and he could not know how diverse our society would become and the richness and challenges that such diversity would bring. These changes will generate new issues into the 21st century. One of the frustrations of working in the independent sector is that working toward effecting change in the lives of people does not lend itself to neat, permanent solutions.

In the following pages, I attempt to summarize the current state of the sector in terms of the issues I identified above and, where possible, point to possible future directions as I see them.

Resources

Even in the most generous of times, voluntary, nonprofit organizations struggle to maintain balanced budgets and address the needs of their clients. Too many do so at the expense of employees, who work for lower wages and benefits than those in the other sectors, and with few opportunities for professional development and growth. Nevertheless, the sector has become a powerful force in our society. Total expenditures of the sector in 1990 were $356.6 billion. When the value of volunteer time is added, the total is $455.2 billion. The sector employed 8.6 million people in 1990, or 6.3 percent of the work force.

The issue of resources has once again become of paramount importance and urgency. In the face of increasing need, as a result of an increase in the numbers of families living in poverty, the rising costs of health care and other services, and following four years of declines in contributions by American households, the sector is now facing draconian cuts in the federal programs that are the source of approximately one-third of the revenues for human and social service programs. In addition to reductions in federal spending in the programs of interest to the nonprofit sector, some programs may be devolved to the states through block grants.

An INDEPENDENT SECTOR study of 108 nonprofit organizations around the country, operating 305 programs representative of the range of services provided by the sector, revealed that the cuts in the House FY 1996-2002 budget would cause severe reductions in services. In order to maintain level services, with inflation at 3 percent, and contributions increasing at 5 percent a year, these organizations would have to increase contributions from private sources by 70 percent over seven years. Given the deepening cuts in the House budget in the years from 2001 to 2002, they would have to increase private contributions by 124 percent.

American households, on average, contribute about two percent of their incomes. Even an increase to the 5 percent that INDEPENDENT SECTOR's Give Five campaign has been recommending as a goal would not yield enough revenues to replace the loss of federal funds. Moreover, higher inflation would erode purchasing power for these organizations.

Our research could not predict what would happen if states do not use the block grants for their original purposes. It is probably safe to assume that some states will use the funds for tax reductions or for the most popular causes and issues. In an election year, some will choose the expedient over what is right.

Ethics, Accountability, Responsibility, Trust

As the independent sector grows in size and impact, it is right that the public, the media, and the government demand more accountability and evidence of effectiveness. A public trust requires the highest standards of ethics and management practices. Nevertheless, each new story of waste, fraud, or mismanagement, even when only a few individuals or organizations are involved, makes us all suspect.

The independent sector has traditionally enjoyed higher public trust than either government or business. Our work on many issues has allowed us to enjoy a halo effect. More recently, we are being called another "special interest" group. In the near future, when nonprofit organizations begin to turn away individuals and families seeking services, I suspect the scrutiny and criticisms will increase in volume.

The sector must lead the way in creating and strengthening a culture of "obedience to the unenforceable," on the one hand, and in getting out the story of the thousands of organizations that do exemplary work under chronic constraints on resources.

INDEPENDENT SECTOR will continue to monitor Congress' actions and oppose onerous reporting requirements. We will also continue to use our meeting ground role to generate dialogue on this important issue, and our Leadership and Management program will continue to promote *Everyday Ethics and A Vision of Evaluation,* tools that can help organizations monitor their ethics and make decisions informed by ongoing evaluation.

We will also continue to work with journalism schools, editorial boards, and journalists to help them increase their knowledge and understanding of the sector. The sector will always be challenged by the need to help the media turn stories about doing good into "news" stories.

Tax Exemption

As the federal and state governments seek to reduce deficits and lower taxes for individuals, nonprofit organizations, especially those with sizable assets, become attractive targets. Terminating the tax-exempt status of some organizations will allow politicians to accomplish several things: increase tax revenues, silence organizations that advocate and lobby, and satisfy the business interests that cry unfair competition from nonprofits.

However, those intent on cutting federal funds for human and social service programs repeatedly state that the nonprofit sector will have to do more in those areas. Organizations that may end up paying taxes will, undoubtedly, be forced to reduce services to clients.

Currently, there is talk simultaneously about a flat tax that will not allow any deductions, and about increasing tax deductions, or enacting tax credits for contributions as a way of increasing incentives. A flat tax that will not allow individuals to deduct their contributions will have a devastating impact on revenues from private contributions. Our research clearly indicates that, while people do not necessarily contribute to get the tax deduction, deductibility affects contributions. The more people can deduct, the more they give because it costs them less to give.

While we welcome any action that will provide incentives for people to increase their contributions, such as a tax credit or full deductibility, we must make very clear that the sector cannot be a substitute for government in seeing to public need. The sector must continue to be the incubator for creative solutions for social problems, the provider of services to those who cannot afford market prices, and the advocate for those without a voice.

Lobbying and Advocacy

One of the most important contributions of the independent sector to society has been its work advocating and lobbying for minority groups, unpopular causes, and the poor and voiceless. There is renewed interest among members of Congress in restricting the right to lobby and advocate for organizations that enjoy tax exemption and receive contributions from the public and philanthropy. These organizations lobby for protection of the environment, workers, and children. Nonprofit lobbying was behind the civil rights movement, help for abused women and children, and quality television programming for children. Nonprofit advocacy changed attitudes toward drinking and driving, and toward smoking and health. The contributions to the strengthening of our democratic traditions, and pushing our country toward health, justice, and equity, to name just a few, are so pervasive that most Americans take them for granted. Recent events indicate that we can lose this valuable function and role of the independent sector.

If nonprofit organizations are not permitted to lobby, it is clear that the poor, the voiceless, and the powerless will remain poor and voiceless and powerless. If the nonprofit sector advocacy voice is silenced, will the foundations that fund them be next? What about socially responsible corporations? If we lose our right to speak up against government actions with which we do not agree, can we hold on to any of our other rights? The constitutional right of organizations to engage in advocacy must be protected and fought for, perhaps again and again.

Technology

The nonprofit sector has never had the luxury of limiting the number of issues that it faces. While we are engaged in coping with budget cuts and declining resources, strengthening our ethical management practices to recover lost trust, educating the public, government, and the media about the sector, and protecting our constitutional right to lobby and advocate, we must also work to gain access to technology. If nonprofit organizations are to continue to improve their ability to provide services and to demonstrate effectiveness, accountability, and responsibility, we must learn to use technology. We must be able to acquire the necessary hardware, software, training, technical assistance, and consulting.

The current thinking in Congress appears to be that market

forces will take care of the problem of technology's accessibility and affordability. But some in the sector think that by the time the market forces take care of the problem, the sector will be years behind. In the meantime, we will not have the benefit of the increased cost-savings and productivity promised by the technology.

Diversity and Community

One of our national strengths is also one of our challenges. Our country enjoys a richness of cultures, languages, races, ethnicities, world views, work and learning styles, and communication styles unparalleled in the world. Unfortunately, too many see this richness as a problem instead of an opportunity. Signs of our fraying sense of community abound. Politicians pander to the fears of those who have been marginalized by the rapid changes in our economy and workplace, and encourage them to believe that the source of all difficulty lies in providing government programs for "them": usually women, the poor, and people of color.

The independent sector must find a way to lead the country in finding ways to make our rich diversity work for us as we work toward "a wholeness that incorporates diversity" and a community that is better and greater than the sum of its parts. If we fail to provide effective leadership, our democracy will continue to be seriously jeopardized.

We must play the role of convener of groups of stakeholders to engage in much needed dialogue about our changing attitudes toward the social contract. We need to help Americans understand that the rugged individualism that made this country the power it is may have been appropriate in an expanding economy and limitless resources. But the new global economy, with the increased interdependence and permeable borders among nations, declining resources, and increasing expectations about standards of living, requires that we learn to live and work cooperatively. We must redefine community to be more inclusive. We must re-examine our values of compassion and fairness and justice.

The independent sector is the only sector that can provide such leadership.

The Decline of Democratic Faith

Jean Bethke Elshtain

Democracy is on trial in America. Experts and ordinary citizens lament the growth of a culture of mistrust, cynicism, and scandal. Although a dwindling band of pundits and apologists insists that Americans are suffering the pangs of dislocation en route to salutary change—even progress—such reassurances ring increasingly hollow. By any standard of objective evidence, the better case belongs to those who point to the growth of corrosive forms of isolation, boredom, and despair; to declining levels of involvement in politics from simple acts like the vote to more demanding participation in political parties and local, civic associations. In short, the better case belongs to those who point to the overall weakening of that world known as democratic civil society.

Social scientists who have researched the sharp decline in civic participation argue that the evidence points to nothing less than a crisis in the forging of bonds of social and political trust and competence. The pernicious effects of rising mistrust, privatization, and anomie are many. For example, there is empirical support for the popularly held view that where neighborhoods are intact, drug, alcohol abuse, crime, and truancy among the young diminish. Because neighborhoods are less and less likely to be intact, all forms of socially destructive behavior are on the rise. Americans at the end of the twentieth century suffer from the effects of a dramatic decline in the formation of social bonds, networks, and trust coupled with a decreasing investment in children. That children, in particular, have borne the brunt of negative social trends can be proved by looking at any American newspaper any day of the week. Family breakdown contributes to violence at unprecedented levels even as it generates unparented children who attend schools that increasingly resemble detention homes rather than centers of enduring training, discipline, and education.

Why is this such a worry? In light of our tendency to hunker down into bristling "identity groups" that claim they have nothing to say to one another, these trends point to a deterioration of the web of mediating institutions. At stake here is the vibrant informal and formal civic associations that democratic theorists historically have either taken for granted as a backdrop or—like Alexis de Tocqueville—have articulated explicitly in exploring the relationship between democracy and the everyday actions and spirit of a people. Democracy requires laws, constitutions, and authoritative institutions, but also depends on democratic dispositions. These include a preparedness to work with others for shared ends; a combination of often strong convictions coupled with a readiness to compromise in the recognition that one can't always get everything one wants; a sense of individuality and a commitment to civic goods that are not the possession of one person or of one small group alone. The world that nourished and sustained such democratic dispositions was a thickly interwoven social fabric—the web of mediating institutions already noted. Tocqueville saw Americans as civically engaged, arguing that: "Americans of all ages, all conditions, and all dispositions constantly form associations." From this associational enthusiasm, currents of social trust and helpfulness flowed; indeed, such social trust no doubt helped to account for the enthusiasm for joining and helping. Other famous visitors to our shores spoke of the "active beneficence" that characterized the American public.

But this public spiritedness is in jeopardy. Our social fabric is frayed. Our trust in our neighbors is slow. We don't join as much. We give less money, as an overall percentage of our gross national product, to charity. Where once rough commitment pertained, now we see "In your face," and "You just don't get it." Perhaps a few words about the trust data are in order. For, as political scientist

Eric Uslaner has pointed out, "When trust is low, interest groups that make non-negotiable demands on politicians have greater leverage." The question, "Do you believe most people can be trusted or can't you be too careful?" was first posed in 1960 in a famous Civic Culture study conducted by Gabriel Almond and Sydney Verba. It has been repeated yearly from 1971 on. In 1960, trust stood at nearly 60 percent. Social trust waned, with some up and down fluctuations throughout the 1960s and 70s; it did a bit of bouncing up in the mid-80s, but in 1993 social trust reached an all-time low: 37.5 percent. When even mainstream social scientists begin to get alarmed, we should perhaps pay attention. The general, widely shared consensus now is that overall social trust is far too low to sustain consensual norms, to generate robust communal action, and to build workable coalitions. This is not good news.

Actually, the ever prescient Tocqueville, in *Democracy in America*, offered foreboding thoughts along these lines. He warned of a world different from the robust democracy he surveyed. He urged Americans to take to heart a possible corruption of their way of life. In his worst-case scenario, narrowly self-involved individualists, disarticulated from the saving constraints and nurture of overlapping associations of social life, would require more and more controls "from above" to muffle at least some of the disintegrative effects of egoism. To this end, civic spaces between citizens and the state needed to be secured and nourished. Only many small-scale civic bodies would enable citizens to cultivate democratic virtues and to play an active role in the democratic community. These civic bodies were in and of the community but were not governmentally derived—not the creatures of the state, so to speak. Tocqueville's fears were not that anarchy would result should this world of associational life weaken but, rather, that new forms of domination might arise. All social webs that once held persons intact having disintegrated, the individual would find himself or herself isolated and impotent, exposed and unprotected. Into this power vacuum would move a centralized, top-heavy state or other centralized and organized force that would, so to speak, push social life to the lowest common denominator.

A recent *New York Times* article on the 1994 campaign reports that "U.S. Voters Focus on Selves, Poll Says," and brings into question the long range effects of this shift on the legitimacy and sustainability of liberal democratic institutions. The *Times* noted a "turn inward" and the lack of any "clear direction in the public's political thinking other than frustration with the current system and an eager responsiveness to alternative political solutions and appeals" (Sept. 21, 1994, p. A21). Based on a *Times-Mirror* survey, manifestations of voter frustration included growing distance from either of the major parties and massive political rootlessness among the young tethered to high rates of pessimism about the future. Most striking was a significant decline in "public support for social welfare programs," although the level of social tolerance for minorities and homosexuals was high so long as one did not have to bear the burden of financial support or direct "hands-on" involvement in the issue (*Times-Mirror Center for the People and the Press* survey, Sept. 21, 1994).

I want to speculate, briefly, on trends that are traceable directly to the collapse of America's social ecology or, alternatively, that helped to bring about the negative developments reported in the *Times-Mirror* survey. One is the tendency to remove political disputation from the political arena into the courts. Thus, Americans have witnessed over the past four decades a tendency to derail public debate by judicial fiat. The second is the emergence of a new form of plebiscitary democracy that reduces voters and legislators alike to passive (albeit angry) consumers or instruments. It is not overstating the case to speak of a "spiral of delegitimation" that has its origins in widespread cynicism about government and politics, the disintegration of civil society, a pervasive sense of powerlessness, and other cultural phenomena.

Political scientist James Q. Wilson argues that one reason Americans are more cynical and less trusting than they used to be is that government has taken on more and more issues that it is ill equipped to handle well: volatile moral questions like abortion and "family values," for example, or some aspects of race relations that treat "blacks" and "whites" as if they were homogeneous interest groups, rather than collectivities themselves divided by regional, religious, class and other lines. These "wedge issues," as political strategists call them, were generated in part by federal courts who made decisions in the 1960s and 1970s on a whole range of cultural questions without due consideration of how public support for juridically mandated outcomes might be generated. Such juridical moves not only froze out citizen debate but deepened a juridical model of politics first pushed by liberal activists but now embraced by their conservative counterparts. Juridical politics is "winner take all" built on an adversarial model. This model, in turn, spurs "direct mail" and other mass membership organizations whose primary goal is to give no quarter in any matter of direct interest to them and to them alone. By guaranteeing that the forces on either side of such issues as abortion—or certain highly controversial mandated "remedies" to enforce racial or gender equity—need never debate directly with each other through deliberate processes and legislatures, the courts deepened citizen frustration and fueled a politics of resentment.

In turn, this politics of resentment tends to reduce legislators to passive instruments of single-issue lobbies and media overkill, thereby deepening the social mistrust that helps to give rise to such efforts in the first place. If one were to revisit the most controversial and divisive issues of the past three to four decades, one would probably discover a dynamic not unlike the one I here describe. At present, aggrieved citizens say, in effect, "Let's take things back," through direct, rather than representative democracy. Indeed, the *Times-Mirror* survey I cited above concluded that the "Perot phenomenon," which speaks to widespread voter anger and resentment, went deeper and was more persistent than experts believed. The director of surveys for *Times-Mirror* professes shock at the "Ross Perot phenomenon" even as the Democratic Party is "depleted and dispirited" and the Republican Party is divided on social tolerance issues. It comes down to this: judicial fiat displaces institutions of constitutional democracy by radically expanding its own mandate into the realm of democratic debate and compromise where things can be worked out in a rough and ready way. In turn, the proclaimed solution to expanded juridical power, plebiscitary or direct democracy, poses a threat of another (albeit related) sort by promoting the illusion that the unmediated "will of the people" will have final say on all issues. Although we are nowhere close to an official plebiscitary system, the trend is disturbing. And the emergence of a sour populism only feeds the conviction that we cannot talk to one another. Paradoxically, in the name of multiculturalism, we seem to be heading toward competing monoculturalisms, with each group playing what political scientists call a "zero-sum game": I win; you lose. Or my group is vindicated; yours is reviled.

The tale here gestured toward is a story of the unraveling of the institutions of civil society, hence the dramatic upsurge in all forms of social mistrust and generalized fearfulness and cynicism, to the current crisis of governing I have called a spiral of delegitimation. Recent studies show that Americans without regard for race "cite the same social problems: crime, poor education, imperiled sanctity of home and family" (Seib and Davidson, 1994, pp. A-1, 6). Not only does this challenge the racialist monocultural insistence that African Americans and whites are entirely separable groups with competing interests as well as identities, it shows that, if anything, African Americans are more insistent that their society faces a crisis in values, beginning with the family, than white respondents overall. But there is less agreement on why things have gone wrong and what can be done to put them right. "More economic opportunity" is noted, vaguely but persistently, as a goal for African Americans, who also express almost no confidence in American legal institutions or politics, yet want "government" to create jobs and opportunities. Whites see a smaller role for government but not surprisingly, given recent developments, neither whites nor African Americans express confidence in the institutions of liberal democratic society. Both groups, in other words, seem ripe for Perot-type "direct democracy" efforts and both seem equally susceptible to the distortion of democratic debate in the hands of media scandal mongers and unscrupulous demagogues. This is a situation begging for a true democratic debate, courageous leadership, wise legislation, and the rebuilding of a sturdy civil society of which nonprofit organizations are a central and indispensable feature.

The sociologist Robert Bellah reports that Americans today

brighten to tales of community, especially if the talk is soothing and doesn't appear to demand very much from them. Yet when the discussion turns to institutions and the need to sustain and support authoritative civic institutions, attention withers and a certain sourness arises. This bodes ill for liberal democratic society, a political regime that requires robust yet resilient institutions that embody and reflect, yet mediate and shape, the urgencies of democratic passions and interests. As our mediating institutions, from the PTA to political parties, disappear or are stripped of legitimacy, a political wilderness spreads. People roam this wilderness fixing on objects or policies or persons to excoriate or to celebrate, at least for a time until some other enthusiasm or scandal sweeps over them. If we have lost the sturdiness and patience necessary to sustain civil society over the long haul, liberal democracy itself—as a system, a social world, and a culture—is in trouble.

References

Seib, G. F. and Davidson, J. "Whites, Blacks Agree on Problems; the Issue is How to Solve Them." *The Wall Street Journal,* September 29, 1994, p. A-1.

"The People, The Press and Politics: The New Political Landscape." *Times-Mirror Center for the People and the Press* survey, September 21, 1994.

"U.S. Voters Focus on Selves, Poll Says." *The New York Times,* September 21, 1994, p. A-21.

Where Have all the People (and Their Dollars) Gone?

Michael Miller

I

"Apathy." After hearing it used to explain low turnout at a meeting or for an election, I've come to conclude it is the label we place on people who don't come to our meetings or don't vote when we think they should. It's a lot easier to call someone "apathetic" than to determine why they aren't participating. This is a form of blaming the victim. A similar kind of blaming the victim takes place in the analysis of shrinking donations to churches and nonprofits. Generally speaking, I think that this kind of analysis misses the point and fails to explain what is really happening.

Having identified "apathy" as the problem, the often suggested remedy is "education" or "motivation." Thus we see numerous programs which seek to educate or motivate citizens to accept their civic responsibilities or to understand their moral responsibility to volunteer time and donate money. These efforts at education and motivation don't work because the educational or motivational agenda isn't informed by the concerns or priorities of those intended to be the "students" or who are presumed to be "unmotivated." Thus the appeals fall on deaf ears.

II

Analysts with a different perspective explain why people don't participate by blaming the system. We can note the systemic reasons given, and give each and all of them their due, and still not understand what is going on. Let me briefly mention some of these systemic reasons.

Average American wage and salary workers are now doing the equivalent of one month more work than they were in 1967. About seven million Americans now work second and third jobs. Add to that increases in commute time. Add to that the scattering of friends who once used to all live in the same neighborhood and now take an hour to visit—and that's when they're considered "local" friends. Add to that school busing if you're a parent who once could participate in the neighborhood school. Time is a real problem for most Americans.

So is money. Since 1973, the real income of most American wage and salary households has only barely inched ahead of inflation. But that's largely because two earners, sometimes working more than one job each, replaced one earner working one job that paid enough to keep a family together. We can note here that half the women who have entered the labor market say they did so as a necessity, not as a choice.

The extraordinary pressures on individuals and families to buy, buy, buy only increase as more time is spent by adults and children watching television. When dominant institutions tell families that they are what they have or what they look like, they soon start acting as if that were true.

Communities—places where people once enjoyed face-to-face relationships that went beyond a hurried nod in the morning or evening—have been undermined by the combination of urban renewal, highways, redlining, employer abandonment and other forces that are familiar to us all.

Candidates for office now measure us with surveys and in focus groups to see what we want to hear, and then tell it to us when they run for office. We are divided up into constituency "segments" and sent carefully crafted direct-mail appeals to our narrowest interests. We are their market, not a serious public to engage in a deliberative process that will give direction to where we are going as a nation and as a people. There is a serious problem with the marketing approach: it fails to tell us what the constraints on elected officials are. Only after they are elected do the politicians begin to tell the public about why promises "x," "y," and "z" can't be realized. (The last candidate to say he would raise taxes was Walter Mondale, and we know what happened to him!) But the politicians can't treat citizens as buyers for too long without a reaction when the product doesn't offer the promised result. The buyers boycott; witness the extraordinary number of Americans who now don't vote.

The nonprofit providers of programs often do meet important needs of clients or beneficiaries. But the professionalization and bureaucratization of many services have created a gap between the client and the provider. Under these circumstances, clients are less likely to participate and to give. Few nonprofits that I know think of those whom they serve as members and really treat them that way.

Add to the pressures of time, money and consumerism the image of American rugged individualism, with all its strengths and weaknesses, and we can easily explain away the problem of declining participation and declining giving.

There is a flaw in arguments that blame the individual and those that blame the system. If we want to get beyond the typical liberal versus conservative arguments, we have to get beyond "blame the victim" versus "blame the system."

III

Aggregate data are useful to observe trends. They don't do too much to explain them. Nor do they allow us to examine exceptions—and it is in the examination of the exceptions to trends that we find clues to what otherwise often appears to be an iron rule.

While most mainline churches, for example, are facing declining attendance and giving, a few are growing. And if we shift our focus to Evangelical and Pentecostal churches, we see many more examples of dramatic growth.

Likewise, twelve-step programs are experiencing vast growth.

So are certain kinds of community organizations—though not others.

Sometimes there is even an exception to the rule of declining rates of electoral participation.

Why?

IV

The organizations with which I'm most familiar, and with which I typically work, are what have come to be known as broadly based community organizations. They are of two types. Some are direct membership organizations. That is, you join them as an individual. The Association of Community Organizations for Reform Now (ACORN) and the affiliates of the Center for Third World Organizing (CTWO) and the Western Organization of Resource Councils (WORC) are examples. Some community organizations are federations of existing groups—typically local religious congregations. Most of these are now associated with one of four national networks, the oldest, most influential and best known being the Industrial Areas Foundation (IAF). Other networks are PICO (Pacific Institute for Community Organizing), Direct Action Research & Training (DART) and Gamaliel Institute; there are regional networks such as Regional Council of Neighborhood Organizations (RCNO) and Organizing & Leadership Training Center (OLTC) as well and some independents. Yet others of these organizations gather around The Midwest Academy, the National Training and Information Center, Grassroots Leadership, and other organizing centers.

Because of another project with which I'm now working, I've also gotten to know a number of Evangelical and Pentecostal pastors and other leaders who have some fascinating stories to tell about what is going on in some of their churches.

I do not hear the leaders of these organizations, particularly some of the denominational leaders and pastors, complain of declining participation or giving. As I've reflected on the hundreds of stories these leaders and their members have told me, I've drawn the following conclusions about civic engagement and giving.

The organizations that command the time and money of their people are organizations that also make demands of their people. In the first place, those who participate in them are members, not clients or beneficiaries. A lot is asked of these members.

In these churches, there are expectations of how members will live. They are challenged to be disciples. They are challenged to act in the world on the basis of their faith. That is how some of the churches connect with the broadly based community organizations. The congregation views the community organization as an extension of itself rather than as an imposition on its members which competes for their time, money and talents. The members are participants in a multiplicity of activities within their congregations. Generally these are organized by a smaller group of unpaid members who have the responsibility for the activity—thus they have an opportunity to learn new skills, gain self-confidence and fill important roles. The members are not consumers of what the pastor, staff and a few activist lay leaders provide. Rather, they are co-creators in the process.

These are frequently tithing congregations: members are expected to, and often in fact do, give 10 percent of their earnings to the church. They give a lot and they get a lot. But it is not only members giving to their churches. I was recently consulting with an organizing effort in which local church leaders (both "mainline" Protestant and evangelical) had to bite the bullet and raise some local funds. They had earlier agreed to assessments of their congregations on an average of several hundred dollars each as an initial dues. But the grants weren't coming in, and the question they faced was whether or not they were going to be able to continue. They asked one another if the organization was important; they reflected on what it meant to their faith; they examined the skills they and their leaders were learning, and the self-confidence that was growing among all of them. When they concluded this evaluation, they came up with different figures. The smallest congregation was to pay $1,000 a year, the largest

$5,000. This kind of dues structure characterizes many of today's institutionally based organizing projects.

In the best of the community organizations, a small organizing staff challenges residents and leaders in low-, moderate-, and middle-income neighborhoods to assume more and more complex roles in their organizations. Homemakers who were nervous when they met their child's third grade teacher now negotiate with mayors. Leaders with GEDs or less formal education research power structure and issues. The skills of planning and running effective meetings are widely learned. Politicians and public, private and nonprofit managers and executives meet with the leaders of these organizations in public accountability sessions attended by thousands of the very same people who were considered apathetic by unknowing observers.

These organizations, and their member groups, are tapping into strong desires that are shared by most people: to be part of something important and bigger than oneself, something that is related to deeply held values and that has to do with the common good; to be in deep relationships with people beyond their immediate families and closest friends; and, finally, to be able to act on issues that directly affect their own lives, and the lives of their families, friends, and neighbors.

Over and over again in my experience as an organizer, it was not what was accomplished "out there" in the world that was most significant to participants—though the external activity is an inseparable, important precondition to what is most important. What is most important to them is that they get to be somebody in their community. Once, I worked in a predominantly Latino community with Latino, Pacific Island, and Anglo lower-income youth and young adults. The community organization for which I was working had a youth employment committee, which later evolved into an adult and youth employment committee. Instead of professional job developers seeking employment opportunities from employers, members of this committee met with employers and negotiated with them. To be one of these negotiators, a person had to attend training sessions and be approved by the committee as one of its negotiators. Jobs were distributed within the committee on the basis of earned "points." Participants got points for the various activities in which they engaged, including research and negotiations. If needed, direct action—including picketing, boycotts, and sit-ins—was undertaken to get recalcitrant employers into good faith negotiations. Points were earned for these activities as well.

I observed that some of the most active members and leaders in the committee were "passing" on some of the best jobs. This meant that instead of taking the job they were letting it move down the ladder of the point list to someone else. I was puzzled, and began asking what was going on. The response was summed up by a young Chicano who said to me, "Mike, I'm never going to get an opportunity to do something like this for my community again. People on the street know me now. They talk about how I led a negotiation to get jobs for our people. I can always get a job."

On another occasion, the Committee successfully negotiated a major agreement, including full-time adult jobs and bilingual services, from the phone company. As we left the negotiations, I turned to the Committee's lead negotiator and said to him, "Wasn't that terrific?" I was referring to the content of the agreement. He replied, "It sure was, Mike. Did you hear that vice-president call me 'Mr. Lopez'?"

When I travel the country now doing research on a report The Aspen Institute has funded, I find similar stories from organizers whether they are working in low- or middle-income communities, and no matter what the color or ethnicity of the people with whom they are working.

A parallel process takes place in electoral politics. The "religious right" best understands this, but it need not be their monopoly. They know that if you tap into deeply felt concerns, give people important roles to play, and select action that can lead to concrete results, people will participate.

V

There is a synthesis of "blame the victim" and "blame the system." Writing of his experience in a Nazi concentration camp, noted psychotherapist Victor Frankl pointed out that we may not be able to choose our circumstances, but we have the freedom to choose our responses to them. That is our individual responsibility. He went on to note that those who didn't psychologically surrender to their situation were also those most likely to survive. Observers of the social scene who argue that people can't abdicate their responsibilities by saying they are victims have an important piece of the truth. But this is not to say, as they sometimes do, that there aren't oppressive or discriminatory institutions in the world. Nor should it be taken to mean that the struggle against oppression is an easy one in which to engage. But part of our human freedom is the opportunity to gather together in voluntary associations and take action to change the system. When the people who are the presumed victims take such action on their own behalf, and on behalf of their families, friends, and neighbors, they will identify what has to be changed in systems. "Blame the system" is no longer in opposition to "blame the victim." Rather, this perspective says that people must take responsibility for their situations, that they cannot simply act and complain as victims. At the same time, this perspective proposes that one of the things the "victims" should do is organize themselves to change those aspects of the system that deny or undermine their humanity. This approach is neither conservative nor liberal. In the sense of "going to the root," it is "radical."

VI

I do not want to suggest that reversing the withdrawal from public life is easy. Rather, it is simple but not easy. Civic engagement ultimately rests on hope. And in our time, hope is a fragile thing. It is particularly fragile if your hope is rooted in democratic ideals. Democratic participation—beyond voting, which is the minimum act of citizenship—ultimately rests on participants finding some connection between what they do and what happens in the world. Regular people (who are often called "ordinary") are unlikely to continue participating in organizations that are committed to democratic values and processes if there is no effect from such participation in civic life, or if things seem worse, not better. They may shift their participation to authoritarian organizations and movements because these alternatives offer easy answers, identifiable scapegoats, and provide the "great leader" as the answer to individual problems. Or, people may continue their participation in escapist churches and movements because these promise a better life in the next world, and urge participants to ignore their fate in this one. But they are not likely to remain engaged in the give-and-take of democratic procedures, compromises, and detail work that accompany our civic life.

While I have painted an optimistic picture of community organizing's ability to produce participation, sustaining that participation depends on two kinds of results.

First, the conditions in which people live have to improve. Their schools, neighborhood safety, physical environments, public services, health and child care, work, and income have to get better as a result of their actions. People will struggle for a better life when their struggles bear fruit. The activists will stay in for the long haul, but they are a distinct minority.

Second, the institutions whose decisions affect the conditions of peoples' lives must become more accountable. The mega-institutions are out of control, including the federal bureaucracy, multi-national corporations, and such multi-national institutions as the World Bank and International Monetary Fund. But this absence of accountability is not limited to the largest organizations. I have seen it in small, so-called "community-based," nonprofit organizations as well. A self-perpetuating board of directors and an executive director with good connections to foundations and government funding sources may be as unaccountable to the neighborhood or constituency that their agency serves as any mega-institution. It doesn't depend on that constituency for its funding, so there is no marketplace accountability; its board of directors is not

elected by the community, so there is no democratic accountability.

VII

How does all of this relate to participation and funding of nonprofit organizations? I am particularly focusing here on nonprofits that seek to serve low- to moderate-income constituencies of
whatever racial or ethnic group. They typically have a self-perpetuating board of directors, are community-based, and are funded
by sources from outside the community that is the beneficiary of
its services. I am not talking about symphonies, operas, museums,
large hospitals, or other large nonprofit organizations.

Strategically speaking, I think the nonprofit organizations serving low- to moderate- income constituencies need to align themselves with the community organizing movement I have been
describing. There are two reasons for such an alignment. First, it
is in the institutional interest of community-based nonprofits to do
so and, second, it is consistent with most of their mission statements and the values that underlie them.

Too often, particularly in low-income communities, the so-
called "agencies" (by which local community leaders mean the typical community-based nonprofit organizations) form a thin buffer
between the people and "downtown." Some have called these
agencies the local arm of "welfare colonialism." The nonprofit
agencies depend on corporate, foundation, and government
sources for their money. There is nothing necessarily wrong with
that. There is something wrong when they claim to speak for
communities that never elected them, and, even worse, when they
oppose efforts to build independent community organizations.
When they oppose such efforts, they hinder the community from
developing the leadership and power to solve its own problems
and to move from dependency to interdependence.

The strategy I'm proposing is directly in the interest of the
nonprofit world, just as it is for the community organizing movement. Speaking recently in San Francisco, James A. Joseph, president of the Council on Foundations, said, "As we once exaggerat-

ed the social role of government, we are now exaggerating the potential of the voluntary sector. In the United States, expressions of altruism are more profound than anywhere in the world but that's small potatoes when you look at the real needs of society." According to the Council, American foundations gave away $10 billion in grants last year to cultural, educational, and service agencies. Individuals gave roughly another $90 billion. But, Joseph said, the federal government budget exceeds a trillion dollars, while state and local governments spend half a trillion.

Contrast what Mr. Joseph said with the now fashionable view, expressed at the same meeting by Mindy M. Lewis, manager of community relations for the Cummins Engine company: "These cutbacks," she said, "can create fertile opportunities. The downside is the loss of government dollars but the upside is an environment ripe for new partnerships." But zero plus zero plus zero still equals zero—no matter how creatively they may be added together. Of course, new partnerships are to be welcomed, but if the partner's cumulative resources (including the time and talents of participants) aren't adequate to do the job, then all concerned are still in trouble.

The pressure to maintain and increase government, corporate, and foundation spending for needed social, educational, and cultural programs will be most effectively mounted by organizations that are not themselves directly dependent on those funds— that is, on strong, independent, community organizations. Similarly, the pressure to reverse the current flow of income and wealth away from the poor, the working class, and much of the middle class toward the upper-middle class and wealthy will most likely come about as a result of political engagement that is outside the parameter of activity for the typical nonprofit organization.

There is no formula for the new alignment proposed here. In some cases, it may mean seeking policy guidance from a membership-run community organization—either informally or by inviting formal representation on a board of directors. It may mean connecting job opportunities in the community-based nonprofit to the community organization. In politics, this is called patronage, and it frequently has a bad name; how-

ever, competent people can be found in many places.
Nonprofits that choose to find competent people from within
the ranks and leadership of broadly based community organizations will have a deeper connection to the community that is
their environment and that they seek to serve. A new alignment could mean contracting with organizing centers to organize program beneficiaries into membership groups that can
have a real voice in nonprofit agencies, as well as becoming
participants in the broader life of their communities. Most of
all, it means seeking and maintaining relationships with independent, bottom-up, grassroots, membership-based, member-
funded community organizations. And there is a bonus in this
deal: this relationship also ensures a much higher degree of
accountability on the part of nonprofits to the communities
they are meant to serve.

There is a great deal of talk about partnerships these days.
Usually the partners are corporations, government, and nonprofit organizations. Absent from the table are the bottom-up community organizations that are, in my view, the country's best hope
for realizing its democratic heritage. For nonprofits, partnerships
with community organizations are essential if the services nonprofits provide are to contribute toward people's independence
and interdependence at the community level rather than making
them increasingly dependent on unaccountable agencies—no
matter how well-intended those agencies may be. This seems so
self-evident that it must be asked why these partnerships aren't
more often formed. The answer is not too hard to find.
Democracy is not a neat, needs-assessment, linearly planned
process. It is a process of conflict and compromise, of give and
take, of sometimes heated argument, and even direct action. For
those who prefer rational planning processes, it is uncomfortable
to live with organizations that may have memberships numbering
in the thousands and that are as comfortable at the negotiating
table as they are on the picket line. But if democracy is one of our
core values, then live with such organizations we must!

There are people in the public, nonprofit, and private sectors
who are coming to see that we cannot continue as a democracy

with institutional structures whose policies pay lip service to "the people" but ignore the democratic voices that come from the bottom up. It is this partnership that is the essential one, both for our shared democratic values and for the immediate interests of the nonprofits.

Hidden Faces of the Nonprofit Sector

William A. Schambra

Five years ago, Deborah Darden and other AFDC mothers in Milwaukee's desolate Parklawn housing project decided to fight back. There wasn't much they could do directly to battle the racism, sexism, and classism that bore down upon them, they had come to realize. But they could take control of their own homes and neighborhood. And so they launched the "Count Me In" Campaign, pledging among themselves to ban alcohol, drugs, and profanity from their homes, to supervise a rigorous homework schedule for their children, to teach their kids to address elders as "ma'am" and "sir," and to develop a right relationship with their God. Today, windows throughout Parklawn sport distinctive "Count Me In" posters, so that other concerned parents know immediately where traditional values are honored. And the mothers are getting their lives together, pursuing education and training, and moving into the job market.

One source of training is Lessie Handy's Professional Receptionist Institute. Two years ago, Ms. Handy realized that she had been "called by God" to train African Americans for office work. From her own experience, she developed an eight-week curriculum, including work with the most widely used computer programs, office etiquette, telephone management, and—the students' favorite—how to deal with an irate customer. To date, she has placed over 120 former AFDC recipients in jobs that pay over $6.00 an hour.

Now advising her on business affairs is Bill Lock. Over ten

years ago, Mr. Lock was asked by the inner city Baptist church where he was a deacon to help them launch a small business incubator in an abandoned factory. Today, Community Enterprises of Greater Milwaukee provides scores of jobs in its eight businesses, which include an electronics assembly firm and a home-based elder-care company. Deacon Lock is now drawing other nonprofits into a loose network of like-minded community groups, all of whom subscribe to W.E.B. DuBois's belief that "we must do for ourselves."

In this introductory session of a conference on the future of the nonprofit sector—where my assignment was to spread before you one of several grand alternative visions—why am I instead introducing you to Deborah Darden, Lessie Handy, and Deacon Lock? Because, I would suggest, they capture far better than any studies or statistics the best hope for that sector's future.

There are, of course, Dardens, Handys and Locks in every low-income neighborhood in America. They are regular citizens, who one day decide they've had enough of the poverty and decay surrounding them, and step forward to do something about it. Some are galvanized into action by the sight of the neighborhood's children stepping gingerly around hypodermics and glass vials on their walk to school. Many have themselves struggled up from poverty or addiction, and know they can help others do the same, because they've "been there." Many feel that they have been called by their God to minister to others, and so their work is infused with spirituality and moral exhortation—not because they wish to "blame the victim," but because, for them, there is no agent of transformation more powerful than the timeless story of the journey from Egypt into the Promised Land, from slavery into freedom, from brokenness into wholeness.

All of them have come to realize that it's pointless to wait passively for the larger economic and political system—for Pharaoh—to rescue them from their plight. And so they have determined to do what they can on their own, relying on whatever resources they can scrounge from their neighbors, from churches, from voluntary associations and local foundations—relying on their own determination to take control of their lives and immediate surroundings once more.

When we talk about the future of the nonprofit sector, however, we don't usually think about Darden, Handy, and Lock. What comes to mind instead are our society's massive, gleaming "service delivery" systems staffed by swarms of credentialed professionals and social science experts, topped by towering, bureaucratic management structures, funded generously by the government as program "vendors." The premise of those systems is that low-income citizens can do precious little for themselves. The problems of poverty, after all, arise from the malfunction or unfairness of distant economic and political megastructures, which only credentialed experts can understand, and only comprehensive national policy can redress.

As for Darden, Handy, and Lock, we have developed subtle ways to dismiss them. They make for interesting or even inspiring "anecdotes," we say, but in the end, they are isolated "charismatic figures." They hardly figure prominently in our hopes for the future of the nonprofit sector. After all, their threadbare carpets are mended with silver duct tape. Their grant applications contain misspellings and don't come with glossy annual reports.

They certainly don't fit neatly into our carefully delineated service categories, but seem to think that drug rehabilitation, family counseling, job training, housing, and nutrition are all part of one thing they may call "restoring the neighborhood." They have no professional training; they've taken no courses in sociology. Indeed, they don't even seem to believe in the redemptive powers of the social sciences, but rather in the redemptive powers of—well, someone they call the Redeemer.

Nonetheless, I would suggest, these groups are in fact the key to the future of the nonprofit sector. For what some take to be a temporary cash flow problem for the social service state reflects, I believe, nothing less than a profound loss of public faith in the progressive vision informing that state. According to that vision, which has dominated the landscape of this century, the coherent local community life of America's earlier days had been destroyed by the centralizing, unifying tendencies of modern technology.

Happily, though, the social sciences—wielded by a powerful

central government—promised to restore a sense of community to America, only now at the level of the nation as a whole. The nonprofit sector would help build the sense of national community by transforming itself from a hodgepodge of parochial, amateurish, church-basement charities into a smoothly humming network of secular, professional social service delivery systems harnessed to national goals, fueled by federal dollars. Scruffy grassroots groups would be replaced by what John McKnight describes as "a comprehensive, multidisciplinary, coordinated, interagency, 'wrap-around' service system"—a sort of "virtual reality" neighborhood—a neighborhood without neighbors.

Behind today's far-reaching discussions about reinvention and devolution, I would suggest, is the profound disillusionment with this model wherever it has prevailed, including within the nonprofit sector. Everywhere we find deep dissatisfaction—not only with government, but with the way we have organized ourselves within civic life as well. Today's decline in voluntarism and private charity, for instance, should come as no surprise when volunteers and contributors are given to understand that they are nothing more than a walk-on supporting cast for the real actors: the experts and professionals.

In the final analysis, the American people are not saying that they wish to replace service providers from Washington with service providers from Sacramento or Springfield—or even from the Salvation Army. They are saying: "Stop treating us as the passive, helpless clients of service providers, period. Start regarding us as citizens who are capable of running our own affairs, our own lives, no matter how poor, benighted, or unscientific you may think we are."

By now it should be apparent that we need to take a new look at Darden, Handy, and Lock. Only in a world of megastructures and macrosystems may they patronizingly be dismissed as pleasant anecdotes. In this time of populist revolution, they must be understood as the very embodiment of the new citizenship impulse. For they are restoring the civic institutions—our families, neighborhoods, churches, schools, and voluntary associations—that once covered the face of our national life, that tackled the most urgent human problems, and that were the first and most important instruments of democratic self-government. They are rebuilding American community the only way it can be done: one neighborhood at a time. Sitting in Deacon Lock's office or Lessie Handy's reception area, Alexis de Tocqueville would know instantly that he could only be in America.

In such a revolutionary period, it would be a grave miscalculation to suppose that the largest question facing the nonprofit sector is, how can we find more resources or volunteers for the present service delivery systems? Puzzling over that question is simply fiddling while Rome burns.

The questions we should be asking ourselves are: What can we do to help Darden, Handy, and Lock do what they do so well? Where are the others like them? How can we encourage and support such neighborhood-based, self-help initiatives—without so corrupting them that they become merely additional "vendors" for the social service state? And how can we recast our understanding of the nonprofit sector, indeed, our science of society, so that Darden, Handy, and Lock are seen to be civil society's vital core, its beating heart, rather than idiosyncratic anecdotes from its periphery?

Were these questions at the center of our concern today, I would suggest that many of the other issues troubling us would resolve themselves. Were our resources—whether public or private—manifestly directed toward supporting the work of Darden, Handy, and Lock, rather than a bloated social service empire, I suspect we would soon find a new spirit of generosity sweeping across the face of this land, among conservatives and liberals alike. And volunteers in the bustling offices of Lessie Handy's Professional Receptionist Institute understand full well that they are a vital part of a vital enterprise, not something underfoot.

In the final analysis, the stories of Darden, Handy, and Lock are classic American stories—classic human stories—that cannot fail to stir our hearts and imaginations, unleash our energies, and summon up the best that is within us. And in the power of their stories to transform us, we glimpse the power of the stories that have transformed them, and that, they would insist, testify to the truth of a realm beyond the human altogether.

The Market Economy, Social Responsibility, and the Future of the Nonprofit Sector

Edward Skloot

Fifteen years ago, in 1980, I was privileged to start a nonprofit consulting firm called New Ventures. It was dedicated to the idea that nonprofit organizations should diversify their revenue sources and earn money as a parallel strategy to seeking grants. At the time, the proposition appeared almost heretical. Although there were numerous examples of commercial activity scattered throughout the subsectors of the nonprofit world, remarkably few people had addressed this development in a sector-embracing way.

The response to New Ventures was gradual and modest. For each museum executive or social service professional demonstrating an interest, many others found the idea of earning income an anathema. For some, the opposition was practical; there were simply too many operating uncertainties. For others, the concern was moral; nonprofits had "no right" to go into business. Overall, one could not discern a surge of interest in the services of New Ventures.

In the last 15 years (and seven since I formally left the firm), commercial activity by nonprofits appears to have grown quite slowly, although there are surely eye-catching exceptions. Some of them are described in the companion paper by Janne Gallagher in this volume.

There are three terms commonly used in the field of non-profit enterprise. The first is "related income." Here, an organization markets goods or services that are "substantially related" (as determined by the Internal Revenue Service) to its tax-exempt mission. Income from these activities, say, tickets sold by the Metropolitan Opera to a performance, are not taxable.

The second term is "unrelated income." This is income from goods or services that is "not substantially related" to the tax-exempt mission of the organization. A case in point would be a health institution that rented its computers to a travel agency that, while booking a small number of trips for the institution, did the lion's share of its sales with people unconnected to it. In this case, rental income would have to be declared and would be taxable under IRS rules. In this essay the focus is on substantially related income, the predominant form of nonprofit enterprise.

The third term, of fairly recent vintage, is "cause-related marketing." Here, a nonprofit, for example a children's charity, links up with a national corporation (usually a national one) that uses the organization's identity and its appealing mission to market products. The corporation contributes to the organization a percentage or agreed-upon amount of the increased sales revenue. The revenue gained by the organization is not generally taxable.

Today few nonprofits summarily reject the opportunity to earn money. But, as a practical matter, most remain stymied about how to build a venture that can actually throw off substantial income. Despite well publicized successes, like the Metropolitan Museum of Art's gift shop, the Children's Television Workshop's royalties on the use of its characters, and the Girl Scouts of America's cookie sales—all deemed non-taxable income by the IRS—commercial activity is a marginal component for most nonprofits. It does not add a great deal of income to their bottom line. Indeed, a successful enterprise of any kind is very difficult.[1]

There are no national or local studies regarding how many nonprofits are actually earning appreciable amounts of money from enterprises like the ones noted above, or the percentage of their budgets provided by earned income.[2] My best guess is that the number of organizations with substantial taxable commercial activity cannot comprise more than 2 or 3 percent of the sector total, and the amount of these revenues, relative to that of the nonprofit sector as a whole, surely is less than 5 percent. Admission tickets to museum exhibitions, tuition at universities, clinical care in voluntary hospitals or counseling sessions at nonprofit mental health clinics[3] are related activities tied to the organization's mission and, accordingly, are tax-exempt.

In recent years, although earned income ventures have not greatly expanded, conflict over the tax-exempt status of nonprofit organizations has. The challenges come mainly from two constituencies. The first is from a number of commercial enterprises, like private health clubs, whose operations may (or may not) be threatened by competition from a related venture of a nonprofit, like a YMCA fitness center.

Proprietary health clubs were a booming industry in the 1980s and were often the new entrant in a local market. As businesses became more competitive, some club owners charged that YMCAs had an unfair business advantage because they were tax-exempt, even though they had provided their services for many years. The clashes reflected increasing permeability of the historic boundaries between the two sectors. Disputes have arisen in other areas too—ranging from testing laboratories to educational institutions —and they continue today.

The second concerned constituency is comprised of cash-starved local governments who see nonprofit venturing and, perhaps, the presence of substantial fund balances, as sources of funds to help close their budget gap. They seek payment for municipal services, like garbage collection, in lieu of property or other local taxes from which nonprofits are commonly exempt. For example, the Mayor of Ithaca, New York recently held up construction permits needed by Cornell University in order to obtain an additional $2 million in contributions in lieu of taxes (*The New York Times,* June 9, 1995). In some states, like Pennsylvania, the conflict over tax-exempt income has been particularly virulent. Several legislative efforts and judicial decisions have begun to specifically define (and restrict) charitable, exempt activity for the purpose of determining taxability.

The Benefits of Nonprofit Enterprise

For many of the early years of nonprofit venturing, the issues were largely internal. Almost no one dreamed of nonprofits competing head-to-head with for-profits. The questions focused on whether it would be "good for" a nonprofit to engage at all in some kind of earned income activity.

Experience has shown that there are several benefits for non-profits that have been willing and able to earn a portion of their income—either related or unrelated (Skloot, 1988). First, and most apparent, is the ability of the organization to increase its operating revenue. The organization will return this as income to subsidize current or new programs. In many cases, the revenue stream will not be great relative to the operating budget of the organization, but, all things being equal, a small gain in operating revenue will be worth it—so long as the risk is not large. Small rewards call for small risks.

The second benefit is that earned income can stabilize an organization's health. Earning income helps to diversify the revenue base of the organization, providing a cushion against the changes in the funding (or the government contracting) climate. Since governments and foundations regularly move in and out of program support, the more legs an organization has upon which to balance its services, the more likely the diminishment or loss of one of them will not damage it. This diversification has particular salience today, as Congress and the President are expected to reduce the funds going to nonprofits through both categorical and block grants to states.

Third, earned income activities can help nonprofit managers improve their skills. In general, ventures force an organization to pay greater attention to the bottom line. The more this business-like mindset permeates an organization's thinking, the more likely it will be that decisions are better informed by reasonable financial (as well as programmatic) considerations. In addition, management information systems may need to be created, or upgraded, to handle ventures—a generalized plus for the whole organization.

Fourth, earning income may bring the organization into a wider circle of expertise and knowledge. For example, borrowing money at commercial rates or obtaining a program-related investment (a soft loan) will inevitably bring an organization into closer contact with banks and other lenders. Occasionally, an equity investor might participate as well. Thus, expansion into the market economy often leads to developing better financial and management capacity and broadening useful contacts.

Fifth, earned income may add a bright sheen to the nonprofit seeking foundation or corporate funding. If an earned income venture is doing well, some funders see this as evidence of managerial skill. Some also discern the possibility that the venture might be expanded in order to compensate when funders leave the field.

Sixth, ventures may help attract board members with skill in enterprise and management. These individuals, who may bring a slightly different focus, can help energize and professionalize an inward-looking board. Such expansion may also lead to finding pockets of support from new donors.

Finally, successful earned income activities can occasionally garner good press. In a world where the media and good publicity are often the validators of success, good news can translate into attention, which can perhaps then lead to financial support.

To be sure, all of these internal benefits do not accrue in equal amounts or over a set time period. They can also disappear rather quickly. Indeed, if an earned income venture does not fulfill expectations, or is an outright flop, it can lead to serious repercussions at the board and staff level. This kind of failure can hurt an organization's financial stability, bloody its public face, and fray the culture of the organization. Precious funds may be siphoned off and management that otherwise might run programs may be distracted, disgraced, or dismissed. These are powerful considerations that should give pause to nonprofit executives thinking of taking the plunge into entrepreneurship.

The Subsectors Tell The Story

Patterns of entrepreneurship vary greatly in the nonprofit world, and we must be careful not to lump all nonprofit organizations together. The fact is, the subsectors of the nonprofit world—like human services, arts and culture, health care, environment, and so forth—are enormously varied. They get their resources from different places, they exhibit varying degrees of independence from the public sector, they are more or less engaged in the market economy, and they have quite distinct corporate cultures. Accordingly, deconstructing the sector is an important first step in evaluating the impact and importance of commercial involvement.

Three subsectors are of particular interest. First is the nonprofit health care subsector, which comprises perhaps half of the total revenue of all nonprofit organizations. It is now so embedded in the market economy that the operations of many nonprofit institutions are increasingly indistinguishable from their for-profit counterparts.

Today, for-profit and increasing numbers of nonprofit health care institutions pay high salaries, use financial incentives to motivate management (and attract enrollees), market their products and services to target audiences, and compete for new and old customers as ferociously as makers of breakfast cereal or pain killers. Further, the health and human service subsectors are presently awash in incentives meant to further promote behavioral and cost containment ends in the service of the bottom line. The more charitable and humane side of service delivery, as well as its inefficiencies, seems to be entering a spin cycle.

Some health organizations have resisted this trend, notably Catholic institutions and those located deep in poorer, urban areas whose links to the marketplace are tenuous. But resistance is increasingly difficult. Those nonprofits that are in strong financial shape are becoming take-over targets of large, for-profit health care companies determined to expand their market reach and profitability.

If corporations want the nonprofits' market, governments

want their cash. Some officials of financially squeezed local governments (noted earlier) have discerned this tilt toward the marketplace. They find in it additional reason to call for the revocation of the tax-exempt status of nonprofit health institutions. Hospitals, for example, are increasingly being asked to demonstrate their "charitableness" in order to retain their tax exemption. In response, they now calculate the percentage of health services they provide to the indigent or difficult to care for in a local community, and use the number to defend their claim of exemption.

While there are no national norms or standards, it is clear that the larger the percentage of indigents served, the more likely it will be that tax exemption will be maintained. On the other hand, it is also true that the larger the number of indigents served, the weaker will be the balance sheet of the institution. Exemption can carry a heavy price.

At the other end of the earned income continuum is the human service subsector. Here, groups engage in very little product or service marketing and their cash-poor customer base makes such prospects unlikely. In the last decade, many human service institutions have become vendors to governments (in New York State they earn $5 billion annually). If anything, these institutions look more and more like public agencies and less and less like free-standing entities of an independent sector. Besides being dependent on government dollars for contracts and reimbursements, they are also more and more subject to government audits, standards of accountability, and local politics. Human service groups are most vulnerable to downturns in public sector support and their low level of commercial activity makes them that much more fragile.

A few subsectors that serve the disadvantaged actually earn income. Low- and moderate-income housing construction, rehabilitation, and management is a case in point. In the last two decades this field has become the domain of nonprofits. This aberrant situation exists because for-profit firms have tried the low- and moderate-income housing market and refused to re-enter it, even with the availability of federal or state subsidy. Venturesome nonprofits, like community development corporations, have filled the vacuum. The income they earn is recycled to support job training, crime prevention, recreation programs, and the like in local neighborhoods. This community payback is a far cry from the way the private sector operates: where profits are commonly taken out of local neighborhoods, not put back in.

Somewhere in the middle of this institutional map is a disparate group of religious and service associations that derive much of their revenue not only from commerce or fees-for-service, but from annual memberships as well. They have recently drawn some public attention for their political activism, but their commercialism has not been well studied. The groups run the gamut from the National Rifle Association and Focus on the Family to the World Wildlife Fund and the American Association of Retired Persons (AARP).

These organizations turn the cash flow of memberships into cash cows. Ventures range from insurance sales by AARP to a panoply of enterprises run by the Christian Broadcasting Network (CBN), whose revenues today exceed 140 million dollars annually. Perhaps one-third of CBN's revenue derives from profit-making enterprises like a jet chartering service, a travel agency, and a television station (*U.S. News & World Report*, April 24, 1995). AARP, CBN and other groups combine membership and enterprise dollars to support their public policy advocacy.

Religious or church-related enterprises have become an especially knotty issue of late. Some in Congress have intervened to stave off IRS tax audits of these ventures. The leaders of these enterprises commonly argue that the audits would breach the wall between church and state, that they constitute a form of harassment, and that the enterprises don't earn income that is "not substantially related" to their mission anyway.

Whether their ventures are related or unrelated, how much they may engage in lobbying or advocacy, and whether they should continue to be tax-exempt are large questions about which we will hear much more in the coming months. The opening salvo was fired by Senator Allen K. Simpson last June when he took AARP to task for its activism and held hearings on its financial and public policy initiatives (*The New York Times*, June 14, 1994). He correctly perceived the connection between tax-exempt organizations with successful enterprises and the ability to mount highly effective advocacy campaigns.

The Commercialization of the Nonprofit Sector

The intersecting concerns about commerciality, the financial needs of local governments, and the advocacy activities of non-profits are converging to build a case for a national review of non-profit status and the tax exemption it confers. But the analysis will be truncated—and inherently misleading—if it glosses over the vastly more consequential matter suggested above: the encroach-ment of the market economy into services traditionally dominated by nonprofit organizations. For-profit health clubs and testing labs are merely the opening wedge of a much more profound trend: market-driven competition that threatens much of the sector's continued existence.

The expansion of for-profit organizations into a traditionally nonprofit universe began in the 1980s with the uniform availabili-ty of Medicare and Medicaid reimbursements and federal funds for capital construction. For-profit hospitals offering short-term care grew by 28 percent and the number of beds they controlled grew by 41 percent. In home health care and outpatient clinic care, for-profits accounted for almost 85 percent of new institu-tions between 1977 and 1987 and nonprofits lost their dominance, dropping from 55 percent of the establishments to 32 percent ten years later.

In social services, including daycare, adoption assistance, fam-ily counseling, and residential care for the disabled and handi-capped, for-profits grew to 48 percent from 36 percent of the field. Only in nursing homes did nonprofit establishments hold their own during the 1980s (Salamon, 1993). But even here, in the '90s, the tide of "for-profitization" has finally come in.

Billions of dollars of third-party reimbursements, public and private, now underpin the finances of America's health and human service institutions, including hospitals, HMOs, mental health and family service clinics, nursing homes, assisted living facilities, foster care, and day care. In each of these areas, for-profit corporations—driven by market opportunity, a stream of reimbursement dollars, and the expectation of profit—are entering and stepping up their competition with nonprofit institutions. For-profit hospital chains, led by the $15 billion Columbia/HCA Healthcare Corporation, are crisscrossing cities and entire regions to stake out turf. The nursing home, home health care, and family services subsectors are not far behind in this escalating scramble for market share.

As a result of the encroachment and the competition it brings, we have begun to see the consolidation and shake out in health care and human services. While some nonprofits face absorption by large national corporations, others are tempted to convert to for-profit status. A number of large HMOs in California and elsewhere have already gone for-profit, and Blue Cross of California is now seeking to convert as well (*The Chronicle of Philanthropy*, June 14, 1994). Family Service America, for another example, is leaving the employee assistance business. It sees the for-profit marketplace as too ferocious to compete in successfully.

Most importantly, all health and human service providers are seeking links with strong, multi-service providers, for-profit or nonprofit. They are aware that single-service institutions will increasingly lose referrals—and financial livelihood—to networks of interconnected service providers. They will keep their referrals (and the money) circulating within the network. Thus, the nature of market forces and competition compels providers in the two sectors to increasingly act like—and even deal with—each other. Nonprofit groups, for better and worse, can no longer stand behind their exempt status and thrive in relative isolation.

In fact, in this increasingly competitive marketplace, nonprofits are in a true bind. They cannot succeed by competing in price: this kind of competition is a self-defeating strategy in the long run, since someone else will inevitably drop his price even lower. In the short run, more often than not, nonprofits are also disadvantaged by the deep pockets and marketing skill of aggressive private sector providers whose size can also help them reduce internal costs—from pharmaceutical purchases to staffing.

Furthermore, they cannot easily afford to refurbish old facilities. Traditionally, they have used their fund balances (retained earnings) and some publicly financed debt to make capital improvements and stay technologically modern. But with local governments now seeking their cut of fund balances and as tax-exempt bond financing loses its local appeal to a tax-wary public, two sources of nonprofit construction funds are drying up. All this will further weaken their appeal to the middle class, who can choose the hospital, nursing home, or clinic they want. This development will force nonprofits to rely on fewer and lesser sources of revenue, further speeding their impoverishment.

It is obvious that a strong dose of competition can productively and usefully weed out poor performers in both sectors. But the further weakening of already vulnerable nonprofit service deliverers can have an obviously damaging effect on the provision of quality service and an equally destabilizing affect on local communities in which they are located (*Business Week*, September 4, 1995). It has been widely documented that nonprofits, compared to for-profits, provide more uncompensated care, offer a much wider range of unprofitable services, and engage in a larger share of the unremunerative research and education programs that benefit all sectors, public and private (Gray; Trocchio).[4] What will happen to these services as competition and consolidation heat up?

The invisible hand of the marketplace is totally impersonal, highly mobile and insensitive to charitable initiative. Its rationale is profit maximization, not human betterment, and it has no motive interest in human equity or community stability. It will accept a social role only if the job is mandated by law or required by regulation. As a nation, we should be less concerned about the rare challenges posed by nonprofit commercialism than about sustaining the institutions that care for the weak, foster strong neighborhoods, and nurture our core values at the same time. We must not forget that it was democracy that created capitalism, not the other way around.

If the cards seem to be stacked against nonprofit providers, they do have one trump card left: their legal status and tax exemption. The rights conferred by nonprofit status may be the most important feature the sector has to preserve its long-term viability. But these rights should be clearly linked to responsibilities in the communities that they serve, for in this connection lies a path of opportunity.

Nonprofit status and tax exemption can help level the competitive playing field, make service to the needy affordable, and define a mission for community involvement. It may entice providers to serve the large and growing underserved portion of the populace, and perhaps even compete with for-profit networks. But we must acknowledge that those who willingly serve the greatly disadvantaged and hard-to-care-for will require both subsidies and incentives in order to keep them in the game and keep quality of services high.

The time has come for the nonprofit sector to embrace and not hide behind a full discussion of its legal status and tax exemption. The sector should deliberately use the endeavor to tease out its rationale for existence in the 21st century. For if exemption merely represents a historically interesting artifact, then the grounds for continuation should be openly questioned.

But we are a long distance from such a conclusion. As a first step, we might well focus the inquiry by asking some useful questions: Why shouldn't nonprofit status and its attendant benefits explicitly require acts of public service? Why shouldn't there be service responsibilities to match the legal rights? Conversely, why shouldn't for-profit providers have a minimum requirement to serve poor patients as their payback for the privilege of receiving taxpayer-derived reimbursements—which are used to further expand market share to the disadvantage of nonprofits? If they refuse, why shouldn't they be taxed to ensure that the services will be provided by others?

Other institutions should ask similar questions. For example, if colleges and universities hold their status tightly, as they do, shouldn't they be compelled to perform at least some community service in their local neighborhoods? Doesn't nonprofit status confer civic responsibilities as well as exemption rights? If not, why have it?

Even more broadly, if it is in our national interest to stimulate and nurture civic participation and strong communities—what is now called "social capital"—what are the long-term implications of the continued expansion of the market economy into the operations of the nonprofit sector? It is erroneous to think that strong communities and helpful social relations can be produced by transient capital and marketplace behavior. More likely, the further erosion of our social capital will march hand-in-hand with the advance of market forces into the nonprofit sector. Shouldn't public policy work to restore this sectoral balance, not thoughtlessly undermine it?

The challenge presented by "for-profitization" is that it can encourage the nonprofit sector to look at itself anew and to frame a set of civic-based service goals and strategies for the 21st century. It might also prompt a searching review by governments, corporations and nonprofits of their respective responsibilities to the American public.

Notes

[1] See "Dead End for Sesame Street," *Business Week,* June 19, 1995, 66-68, which enumerates some of the difficulties and complexities one nonprofit subsector, public television, faces in becoming more entrepreneurial.

[2] Professors Lester M. Salamon and Richard Steinberg have done the best work on capital flows and on enterprise. See Salamon's "The Dynamics of Nonprofit Finance," and Steinberg's "Nonprofit Sources of Earned Income," both prepared for an Aspen Institute conference on "Financing the Nonprofit Sector: New Directions for the 21st Century," December 1994.

[3] This view seems to differ from Professor Salamon's. In his authoritative "The Marketization of Welfare: Changing Nonprofit and For-Profit Rules in the American Welfare State," he charts the significant rise of fees and sales as the principal source of revenue growth in the 1980s for nonprofits. I agree. My purpose is to define what is/is not "substantially related" in the tax code. See *Social Service Review,* March 1993, 17-39.

[4] The Trocchio paper discusses numerous federal and state studies on this point. Gray has written widely on this subject.

References

"Balance Sheets That Get Well Soon." *Business Week,* September 4, 1995, 80-84.

"Charities Win, Lose in Health Shuffles." *The Chronicle of Philanthropy,* June 14, 1994, p. 1.

"Dead End for Sesame Street." *Business Week,* June 19, 1995, 66-68.

"Dispute Over Taxes and Building at Cornell University is Resolved." *The New York Times,* June 9, 1995, p. A25.

Gray, B. H. "Why Nonprofits? Hospitals and the Future of American Health Care." *Frontiers of Health Services Management,*1992, 8(4), 3-32.

"On God's Green Earth." *U.S. News & World Report,* April 24, 1995, 31-32.

Salamon, L. M. "The Dynamics of Nonprofit Finance." Paper presented at the Aspen Institute Conference, "Financing the Nonprofit Sector: New Directions for the 21st Century," December 1994.

Salamon, L. M. "The Marketization of Welfare: Changing Nonprofit and For-Profit Rules in the American Welfare State." *Social Service Review,* 1993, 67, 17-39.

"Senator Challenges the Practices of a Retirees Association." *The New York Times,* June 14, 1994, p. 1.

Skloot, E. *The Nonprofit Entrepreneur,* New York, 1988.

Steinberg, R. "Nonprofit Sources of Earned Income." Paper presented at the Aspen Institute Conference, "Financing the Nonprofit Sector: New Directions for the 21st Century," December 1994.

"Forced Marriage of Medicaid and Managed Care Hits Snag." *The New York Times,* August 28, 1995, p. Bl.

Trocchio, J. "The Case for Not-for-Profit Healthcare." The Catholic Health Association, Washington, DC, unpublished paper.

"Turning to Charities For Taxes." *The Chronicle of Philanthropy,* May 18, 1995, p. 1.

Peddling Products:
The Need to Limit Commercial Behavior
by Nonprofit Organizations

Janne G. Gallagher

Recently, the McDonald's Corporation and Georgia Tech announced a 5.5 million dollar corporate sponsorship deal. In return for its "contribution," McDonald's will get to put the golden arches on the floor of the Georgia Tech coliseum, as well as on all tickets and game programs. McDonald's also will receive exclusive rights to supply all coliseum food and beverages from one of two on-campus McDonald's restaurants that will be designed with a "Georgia Tech" decor. Finally, the one-block area of the campus that contains the university's athletic facilities will be formally known as the "McDonald's Center at Alexander Memorial Coliseum" (Blumenstyk, 1995; Streckfus, 1995).

This anecdote exemplifies what some critics argue is growing commercial behavior by charitable organizations. Other examples abound. The purpose of this paper is to discuss the issue of commerciality in the nonprofit sector, suggest some causes, and raise some concerns about its impact on the future of the nonprofit sector.[1]

What Is Commerciality?

"Commerciality" is a word people use to refer to several different types of behavior by nonprofits. Most narrowly, it means only a nonprofit's non-exempt, unrelated business activities. A wider definition includes exempt, unrelated activities in general and certain types of fundraising in particular. Finally, small business and academic critics use the term "commerciality" to describe the revenue a nonprofit earns from providing services that further its exempt mission.

This analysis focuses first on the problem of commerciality as it relates to how an organization carries on the activities that further its exempt purpose. Questions of whether or not a particular activity is in fact "related"—in other words, whether it substantially furthers an exempt purpose—are beyond the scope of this paper.

Following the discussion of commerciality in related activities, the paper considers commerciality in the context of two controversial, or at least contested, methods for realizing income from an unrelated activity. The first is royalty income from an unrelated trade or business, including royalties based on mail list transactions. The second is the fundraising technique known as corporate sponsorship.

Commerciality in the Conduct of Related Activities

The first aspect of commercial behavior that merits discussion concerns the extent to which charities rely on income from fees and other charges for goods and services that substantially further their exempt purpose. Since commerciality in the conduct of related activities seems to be a problem primarily for charitable organizations rather than the larger group of nonprofits, this part of the paper deals only with charities.

There is nothing novel about a charity charging something for its services. Charges and fees take many forms, ranging from college tuition to museum admissions. Nevertheless, the fact that charities receive part of their income (and often quite a substantial part) from charges and fees is often overlooked in public debate over the proper role of nonprofit charitable organizations, as many people's instinctive reaction is to associate the term "charity" with free goods and services.

Charities operate in a complex market, supplying goods and services that generally are also available from profit-oriented businesses and often from government. Religious institutions, of course, are wholly within the nonprofit sector and education is largely, although not entirely, the province of governmental bodies and nonprofits. However, health care and human services all have for-profit counterparts, and even educational and religious institutions offer some services, such as publishing, that are potentially competitive with businesses.

Critics argue that many nonprofit institutions are relying more heavily on fees for service. It is true that some nonprofits, such as human service organizations, have increased fee income in response to cuts in government support, although they have increased their support from donations as well. Others, such as hospitals, have come to rely almost entirely on fee income, largely due to the availability of reimbursement under Medicare and Medicaid. Data analyzed by Hodgkinson and her colleagues (1992, Table 2.1) show that private contributions accounted for just under 60 percent of nonprofits' current operating expenditures in 1960. By 1990, that figure had dropped to 31.5 percent.[2] As nonprofits increase their dependence on fee income, they become more difficult to distinguish from their for-profit counterparts and the justification for tax exemption and other special treatment becomes harder to explain.

Background

There has been vigorous debate for more than 15 years about whether some charities should pay tax. The extreme position, articulated by organizations such as the Business Coalition for Fair Competition, would classify as commercial any activity that has a for-profit counterpart. Nonprofits would be barred from claiming tax exemption or any other special privilege for their "commercial" activities. Complaints of "commercial" behavior point to university research and testing services, college bookstore computer sales, nonprofit and governmental child care services, YMCA fitness activities, museum stores, and a host of other typical nonprofit services. Ideally, small business advocates would like to bar nonprofits from providing any service that can be obtained from a private supplier, although they would allow nonprofits to continue to serve a narrow range of people who cannot pay or are otherwise undesirable customers ("Business Group Proposes...," 1990).

Hansmann's (1980) distinction between "donative" and "commercial" nonprofits is well known and underlies many suggestions that "commercial" nonprofits should be reclassified as taxable corporations. Too often, however, Hansmann's caution that these should be considered polar or ideal types is lost in this debate. Bennett and Rudney (1987) take the position that commercial nonprofits should be taxed. They define a commercial nonprofit as one that provides goods or services that are available on the private market, unless those goods and services are offered at least 50 percent below cost to target individuals or groups deemed charitable. To retain exemption, charitable contributions would have to form at least 50 percent of the charity's revenue base.

More recently, Colombo and Hall (1995) argue that tax exemption should be limited to nonprofit organizations that can meet a certain threshold of support from charitable contributions. They suggest that contributions should make up about one-third of gross revenue, measured as a four-year rolling average. They allow charities to include the value of volunteer services and the prorated value of capital contributions in calculating their average annual support. However, they also suggest that departures from the one-third support level might be justified. One such suggested departure recognizes that higher education would have trouble meeting the test and recommends lowering the threshold to between 10 percent and 20 percent for such institutions on the basis that their history of exempt status justifies a lower burden of proof that they are worthy of exemption. They also suggest requiring a higher level of support, perhaps 50 percent, for property tax exemption.

State and Local Efforts to Tax Charities

While the unfair-competition advocates have been largely unsuccessful in their efforts to advance their agenda, the need for new sources of revenue is driving local elected officials in the same general direction. Pennsylvania has been the chief battleground for this debate. A 1985 decision by the state supreme court, *Hospital Utilization Project v. Commonwealth,* established five tests for charitable property tax exemption. To be an "institution of purely public charity," an organization must: i) advance a charitable purpose; ii) donate or render gratuitously a substantial portion of its services; iii) benefit a substantial and indefinite class of persons who are legitimate subjects of charity; iv) relieve the government of some of its burden; and v) operate entirely free from private profit motive.

Subsequent decisions by the state's intermediate appeals court used these five tests to advance the court's view that exemption should be limited to a narrow range of organizations that primarily serve the poor with donated resources. The Commonwealth Court gave three major reasons for denying charitable tax exemption: first, that based on the particular facts, an organization did not make a bona fide effort primarily to serve the poor; second, that an organization that regularly realizes a surplus from operating income possesses a private profit motive; and third, that an organization that is substantially funded by government cannot be said to relieve a government burden.

Cities, counties, towns, and especially school boards are using the ambiguities inherent in the five-part test to extort payments in lieu of taxes from local nonprofits. Leland (1995) found that at least two-thirds of Pennsylvania counties have sought or are seeking taxes, payments in lieu of taxes, and voluntary contributions from nonprofits. Various reports indicate that hospitals have been settling challenges to their tax-exempt status by agreeing to make payments in lieu of taxes that equal 25 percent to 50 percent of the tax that would otherwise be due. Other types of organizations also are entering into settlement agreements due to the high cost of litigating tax exemption cases and the uncertain state of Pennsylvania law on charitable tax exemption. A recent editorial in the *Pittsburgh Post-Gazette* described the process as a "shakedown of nonprofit institutions," and likened it to piracy on the high seas.

There are some signs that Pennsylvania's courts may be retreating from their strict scrutiny of charitable tax exemption. The state's supreme court placed some limits on the Commonwealth Court in the *St. Margaret Seneca Place* decision in 1994. That case helped resolve three major issues raised by the five-part *Hospital Utilization Project* test. First, it now is clear that an organization that receives government funding can relieve a government burden, at least where the government funding does not fully cover cost. Second, an organization may charge some individuals more than the full cost of services and use the surplus to cover losses from individuals who cannot afford the full amount. Third, "gratuitous" care is not limited to services provided absolutely free of charge, as some governments have argued, but includes the value of subsidies provided to those who can pay part of the cost.

More recently, the Commonwealth Court ruled that an independent college met all five of the tests in an opinion that made clear that the definition of charity is not narrowly limited to services to the poor (*City of Washington v. Board of Assessment Appeals,* 1995). The court also ruled that charities relieve a government burden when they reduce public demand for services that government elects to provide, as well as those that it is legally obligated to offer to all; that an institution that is open to all benefits a charitable class; and that an institution may refuse services to some who can afford to pay as long as it subsidizes a significant portion of its services.

Local governments outside Pennsylvania also are focusing on the extent to which charitable institutions should be fully exempt from property tax. Cities like Boston, New Haven, Philadelphia, Wilmington, and Washington, DC, have faced a steady erosion of their property tax base as commercial businesses have left for lower-tax areas and residents have moved to the suburbs. Government is often the largest property owner and the largest employer in many older cities, followed by some larger nonprofits such as universities and hospitals. For example, five of Philadelphia's ten largest employers are governments, four are nonprofit educational institutions, only one is a business (City of Philadelphia, 1994, Ex. 2).

Boston led the way in efforts to collect in lieu of tax payments from city nonprofits. The so-called "Boston plan" seeks payments in lieu of taxes from nonprofit property owners whenever they attempt to take currently taxable property off the tax rolls or when they request city permits and waivers to expand or improve their current property. The city advocates a loose formula for determining payments that considers such factors as the cost of providing city services, the organization's ability to pass along the cost of payments to the beneficiaries of its services, and the extent to which the organization's services benefit city residents. Private nonprofit organizations own about 9 percent of Boston's property (Tax-Exempt Property Steering Committee, undated).

Hospitals as Commercial Institutions

Hospitals are a prime target for local governments seeking additional revenue. Largely this is attributable to pragmatic considerations: nonprofit hospitals possess substantial financial resources, they have become less able to muster local political support, and they have less incentive to resist demands because they can pass tax payments and in lieu of tax payments through to third-party insurers and the federal government. That hospitals seem to be relatively easy targets for local politicians reflects what Gray (1991, p. 65) points to as the growing similarity between for-profit and nonprofit hospitals, including heavy reliance on revenues from sale of services, dependence on economic performance for gaining access to capital through the bond market, the decline of local control due to the rise of multi-institutional systems, and the proliferation of hybrid for-profit/nonprofit organizations.

Local officials look at hospitals and see institutions with multi-million dollar budgets, almost all from payments for services. They see large salaries being paid to hospital administrators, but very little evidence of free care and other programs that benefit city residents and reduce the government's health care burden. They see a complicated pattern of subsidiaries and holding companies. In short, they see very little evidence of differences between tax-exempt hospitals and their for-profit counterparts. Gaul & Borowski (1993, p. 42) provide one example:

> Today Graduate Hospital [Philadelphia] is part of a sprawling $400 million health-care conglomerate that includes seven hospitals, a profit-making HMO, dozens of subsidiaries, fifty-three hundred employees, a well-paid executive staff, and lavish headquarters in a renovated gothic church.
>
> Donations, once a hospital mainstay, account for less than 1 percent of Graduate's revenue now. Most of its money comes from fees the hospital charges, just like any commercial business. And there is relatively little charity. Less than 3 percent of its $120 million budget in 1990 went to providing free medical treatment.

Several of these factors are worth dwelling on, at least briefly, as they relate to commerciality. The most important is the decline in the importance of contributions as a source of hospital operating revenue. Gray (1991, pp. 67-68) points out that increased reliance on the sale of services has important consequences in how a nonprofit views itself and the world. Hospitals begin to use business terminology and business techniques like marketing and advertising, and to think in competitive terms. In short, hospitals become more commercial as they become more dependent on the market.

Another factor in the growing commerciality of hospitals is the use of tax-exempt bonds financing in place of charitable contributions and government grants as a source of capital funds. The federal government once made direct construction grants to nonprofit hospitals with accompanying requirements for community services and charity care. Today's reimbursement is through the inclusion of capital outlays in cost factors for determining reimbursement and through access to tax-exempt bonds. Since most for-profit financing also comes from debt, not equity, the only substantial financing difference between for-profits and nonprofits is the tax-exempt nature of nonprofit bonds. Moreover, while federal grants emphasized community service, lenders are concerned with risk and return. According to Gray (1991, pp. 71-72), evaluating creditworthiness "penalizes the provision of unprofitable services and care for uninsured patients, creating a double bind for institutions that try to adhere to the charitable aspects of the traditional mission of hospitals."

A third factor contributing to commercial operations is the growth of the hospital chains that are replacing independent community-based institutions. Incorporating hospitals into larger groups removes an important aspect of the community control that is provided by local boards empowered to make corporate decisions in the community interest.

Finally, one cannot ignore the tremendous downward drag created by the need to compete with for-profit institutions. Providing uncompensated care or other unprofitable services becomes more difficult as competitive pressures intensify, particularly when the institution has no substantial alternative source of revenue. Where cross-subsidization from paying patients once allowed nonprofit hospitals a degree of freedom to carry on charitable activities, the increasing vigilance of third-party payers is closing off this source of surplus revenue.

Nonprofit hospitals did not set out willy-nilly to become commercial institutions. Government policy, especially since the early 1980s, has been firmly based in an ideology that favors competition and market-based systems as the solution to societal problems. This ideological perspective created a set of payment structures that placed little or no value on maintaining nonprofit structures for service delivery. These policies, including particularly generous Medicare reimbursement policies, encouraged the rapid entry of for-profits into the provision of health care services. They are at work today in other areas, including the provision of human services.

Short-sighted tax policy also contributed to the creation of the present widespread network of for-profit health care providers. As exemplified in the *Sound Health Association v. Commissioner* case (1978), the Internal Revenue Service strenuously resisted early efforts to form nonprofit health maintenance organizations. It also has taken a dim view of exemption for alternative forms of health care delivery, such as ambulatory care centers. While not wanting to underestimate the difficulties involved in ensuring that physicians do not benefit impermissibly from various forms of health care delivery, it is not difficult to imagine a different outcome that began with the premise that there was value in protecting nonprofit delivery of health care services.

As noted earlier, local elected officials have made hospitals a prime target of their quest for in lieu of tax payments. State legislators and regulatory officials also have been looking at hospitals. Their focus largely has been on the provision of charity care, but they generally have not succeeded in mandating any requirement that hospitals would have much trouble meeting. Texas legislation is the most stringent, but even those requirements should be easily met, although with a substantial increase in paperwork. Nonprofit hospital associations, particularly the Catholic Health Association, have been exerting leadership in emphasizing community service and helping nonprofit hospitals document what they are doing, but the trend is in the direction of for-profit takeovers and we may be witnessing the collapse of our nonprofit hospital infrastructure.

Standards for Charitable Tax Exemption

While there are substantial difficulties inherent in imposing a specific commerciality test as a condition for obtaining charitable tax exemption, still there are certain standards that could provide an adequate basis for distinguishing charitable organizations from their business counterparts. These characteristics are ones that are not normally embodied in the operation of commercial businesses and their presence in a nonprofit should help ensure that charities do not become "commercial" at their core.

First, no one should profit from a charity. Executive compensation must be reasonable and based on appropriate standards. Compensation arrangements should be fully disclosed, appropriately taxed, and capped to prevent unjust enrichment. A question that needs to be addressed is the extent to which the reasonableness of compensation should be judged based on a market that includes for-profit as well as nonprofit providers. It is possible to theorize either that charities are best served by being able to compete for the best possible talent or that charities are better served by individuals willing to accept lower compensation because of their personal commitment to furthering the charity's mission.

Second, voluntary contributions should be part of a nonprofit's revenue base. Like Colombo and Hall (1995), I include volunteered services and the prorated value of capital contributions in my definition of voluntary contributions. Unlike Colombo and Hall, I would include some forms of government support as contributions. And unlike Colombo and Hall, I am not prepared to venture specific percentage tests. Existing case law suggests that courts traditionally have been satisfied with levels far below Colombo and Hall's proposed one-third, perhaps on the order of 5 to 10 percent. However, contributed support needs to be high enough to be significant and certainly higher than the reported 0.5 to 2 percent for hospitals.

Third, some part of what charities do must involve an uncompensated gift. Gifts can be many different things, including reducing or waiving customary charges, serving people who have trouble finding service elsewhere, and providing below-cost services to the community as a whole or to specific groups.

Fourth, charities should base their decisions about their activities primarily on community need, not economic return. This does not mean that charities should ignore economic return. In fact, some market discipline is likely key to helping ensure that charities provide quality services. It does mean that charities can be expected to take more risks than a comparable business and that they will choose to provide some unprofitable services.

Finally, charities should be governed by volunteers. I believe the question of volunteer governance is central to the existence of charitable organizations. Some argue that volunteer requirements for boards discriminate against low-income individuals who cannot afford to donate free time. Others find this argument patronizing. Some believe that large institutions that must manage substantial assets require paid trustees to assure that they will expend the necessary time and effort. Yet many well-managed, large institutions have volunteer boards. Again, these are questions worth exploring.

Some of these characteristics, especially the bar on private benefit, are embodied firmly in both federal and state law governing tax exemption. Others, such as the characteristic of support from voluntary contributions, can be found in the law of some states. Some, such as the characteristic of volunteer governance, represent the practice of most charitable nonprofits and the standards of watchdog agencies like the National Charities Information Bureau.

Charities must walk a careful line, balancing their commitment to their missions against the need for revenue streams that are adequate to the task. Charities that become too much like businesses risk loss of public trust and support. Government should play a dual role in helping charities keep their balance. First, government policy should explicitly encourage maintenance of a charitable infrastructure in key areas where charities have been traditional service providers. Policy makers should weigh the infrastructure impact of changes in government payment systems, such as the accelerating shift from grants to vouchers (Salamon, 1989) and of changes in methods of service delivery, such as the shift from inpatient to outpatient medical care. Second, lawmakers should tailor the laws and regulations governing charitable tax exemption to encourage noncommercial behavior, while recognizing charities' need for a balanced and reliable revenue stream. For better or worse, the law of charitable tax exemption remains the principal external constraint on charities' behavior (Simon, 1987). In the diverse world of nonprofits, strict percentage support tests are unlikely to work fairly to accomplish this task. But some states have successfully applied the general principle that charities should demonstrate some support from voluntary contributions and some gift to the community to identify and tax charities that have become functionally indistinguishable from businesses.

Commerciality in the Conduct of Unrelated Activities

Most charities engage in some activities that do not directly further their charitable purposes. There is a tendency to equate unrelated activities with activities that produce unrelated business taxable income. However, the two are different.

Nonprofits carry on a variety of activities that do not directly further their exempt purposes in order to raise money, to minimize losses, and as a matter of convenience. Charities actively manage investment portfolios. They rent excess space in buildings that they own. They operate restaurants and cafeterias for the convenience of their employees, members, students, or patients. They engage in a host of fundraising activities from operating thrift shops to church bake sales. Generally these activities, although unrelated, are exempt from federal income tax though most are intended to make a profit.

Unrelated activities leading to taxable income, in the classic sense of ownership of a macaroni factory, appear to be relatively rare. There are several reasons for this, including the availability of alternative nontaxable investments and the general practice of establishing subsidiaries whenever a nonprofit is engaged in a substantial and profitable unrelated activity that is not exempt from tax. This paper does not address the kinds of commercial activities that are concededly charitable. Rather, it focuses on two specific issues at the margin: unrelated activities that may not be taxable because the nonprofit's compensation is in the form of a royalty and activities argued to be exempt because they are not businesses at all, but merely the solicitation and receipt of a charitable contribution.

Royalties

An important modification to the unrelated business income tax excludes all royalties from the definition of unrelated business taxable income (Section 512(b) of the Internal Revenue Code). A royalty is any payment for a right to use intangible property.

Royalty payments for licensing the use of their names and logos on commercial products have become an important source of income for many well-known charitable organizations such as Children's Television Workshop and The Williamsburg Foundation. However, the practice continues to provoke controversy. One recent example is an agreement under which The Arthritis Foundation licensed the use of its name and trademark to Johnson & Johnson Co. for use in marketing a line of pain reliever products. Critics such as Sheppard (1994) focused on The Arthritis Foundation's apparent endorsement of a particular brand of pain relievers, despite a lack of real differences from competitors' products and a cost that was higher than effective generic alternatives.

While the Internal Revenue Service apparently concedes the exempt status of royalty arrangements that involve only the use of an organization's name and logo, it has been locked in combat for several years over the taxability of income from merchandising arrangements that also include use of an organization's mailing list. Many commercial organizations have reached arrangements with charities under which they market products and services, such as credit cards and long-distance telephone services, directly to a charity's supporters with the charity's endorsement in the form of use of its name and logo.

The Tax Court has taken the position in the cases of *Disabled American Veterans v. Commissioner* (*DAV* 11) (1990) and *Sierra Club, Inc. v. Commissioner* (1993), that mailing lists are intangible property and that payments for their use are excludable from income as royalties. A more recent ruling in the *Sierra Club* case (1994) held that income from affinity credit card arrangements also is exempt as a royalty payment. The Internal Revenue Service has not conceded these issues. It has appealed the *Sierra Club* decisions and is continuing to argue that mail list rentals and exchanges produce taxable income (Internal Revenue Service, 1994).

Legislators also are expressing concern about these practices. Sen. Alan Simpson (R-WY) held hearings in June 1995 to look into royalty arrangements by the American Association of Retired

Persons (AARP), which is heavily dependent on product sponsorship arrangements.

There generally is little doubt that most of these types of marketing arrangements do not substantially further a nonprofit's exempt mission; the nonprofit's income is protected from tax only because of the royalty exception. The commerciality difficulty lies in the organization's implied endorsement of the product or service being marketed, leading to the question whether it is reasonable to continue to exclude royalty income from taxation when the licensing arrangement helps a commercial business sell products and services.

One exception may be nonprofits that reach marketing agreements with commercial businesses for the sale of products, such as reproductions of selected works from a museum collection, where the sale would be considered substantially related, and so exempt, if the museum sold the items directly. There seems little reason to penalize a nonprofit for electing a licensing arrangement as an alternative to accepting the risk and expense of marketing the product itself.

Corporate Sponsorship

The commercial aspects of fundraising are multiplying. Besides corporate sponsorship, which is the focus here, there are allegations that some commercial fundraisers create or take over charities and use them to raise funds that are used primarily to pay for the fundraiser's services (*United Cancer Council*, 1993). Gambling events sponsored by nonprofits also raise commerciality issues, particularly when the events are operated by commercial enterprises with charities receiving only a small percentage of the profits.

Public recognition of generous benefactors probably has at least as ancient a history as tax exemption and has a variety of good effects as well, including encouraging others to be generous. However, there is a growing perception that business giving is being robbed of its donative component by hard-nosed calculations of how to maximize the donation's marketing impact. Martin

Grenzebach (1995, p.1), chair of the AAFRC Trust for Philanthropy, said recently: "Traditional giving, directed by a philanthropy staff and the interests of exec [sic] officers, is giving way to more strategically observable programs overseen by financial officers and housed in marketing and public affairs departments."[3]

People do make charitable gifts from a variety of motives that range from the disinterested generosity of the anonymous donor to the desire to receive the public approbation that results from public acknowledgment of a generous contribution. The difficulty with respect to commercialism arises chiefly when the donor is a business rather than an individual, and as the dynamic of the gift moves along a continuum from simple acknowledgment of the business to conditioning the gift on the nature and extent of the recognition the business is to receive.

The prevalence of corporate gifts and their importance as sources of revenue make it particularly difficult to create appropriate rules distinguishing acknowledgments from bargained-for advertising. To date, the Internal Revenue Service's efforts to make such rules have been a notable failure, a failure that is due in large part to political intervention by those charitable organizations that have negotiated the most complex agreements and that stand to lose the most if sponsorship income is taxed.

The Mobil Cotton Bowl sparked the Internal Revenue Service's unsuccessful effort to characterize certain corporate sponsorship income as taxable advertising income. The IRS pointed to several characteristics of the agreement between Mobil and the Cotton Bowl that it believed evidenced a bargained-for exchange in which Mobil paid the Cotton Bowl in order to receive a measurable level of recognition as the Cotton Bowl's sponsor. These included changing the name of the event from the Cotton Bowl to the Mobil Cotton Bowl, requiring that the Mobil name and logo appear in all press releases and be displayed prominently on the playing field, requiring that Mobil's commercial messages be displayed on the scoreboard and broadcast over the public address system, and linking the size of the sponsorship payment to the size of the television audience (*Tax Monthly for Exempt Organizations*, May 1992).

To clarify its ruling in the Mobil case, the IRS issued a set of proposed audit guidelines outlining specific criteria it would use to distinguish bargained-for exchanges from legitimate recognition of corporate contributions (Internal Revenue Service, 1992). The guidelines stated that the IRS would examine sponsorship agreements on a case by case basis, looking at issues such as the value of the exposure the donor receives, linkages between the amount of the donation and the amount of media coverage it receives, whether the recipient provides incidental services, such as tickets to the event and special seating, and the prominence and prevalence of the display of the donor's logo. The IRS attempted to allay the fears of smaller groups by announcing an "audit tolerance" under which small local organizations run mainly by volunteers would not be at risk for having their corporate contributions analyzed for the existence of a return benefit.

Effective lobbying, primarily by nonprofit sports organizations, led the IRS to withdraw the audit guidelines and propose a set of rules that are tolerant of most corporate sponsorship activities (Internal Revenue Service, 1993). While these rules are not yet final, both the IRS and nonprofits are using them as guidelines; some critics argue that as a result sponsorship arrangements are moving closer and closer to marketing agreements. They point to universities that are giving soft drink manufacturers the exclusive right to sell products on their campuses and the apparent acquiescence by the IRS in the argument that college stadium scoreboard advertising is nontaxable rental or royalty income (*Tax Monthly for Exempt Organizations,* April 1994). And, as noted in the introduction to this paper, at least one university has renamed part of its campus.

Most of these deals have direct commercial counterparts. Many companies that pay college athletic associations to change the name of their events and display advertising on their scoreboards enter similar arrangements with commercial sports arenas. The District of Columbia's proposed new downtown arena apparently will be named for MCI Corporation. The Washington, DC area already has the USAir Arena in Largo, Maryland. The challenge in regulating or limiting this behavior is twofold. First, nonprofits will not lightly give up or limit the substantial income they receive from these sponsorship arrangements. Second, it is extraordinarily difficult to draft rules that adequately distinguish the innocuous from the harmful.

Federal funding cuts will only step up the pressure for non-profits to seek corporate sponsorship income. The Public Broadcasting Service already has asked Congress to let it run more elaborate messages from its corporate underwriters. While there still would be some differences between commercial advertising and "enhanced underwriting," the already blurry distinction would fade even further. PBS acknowledges the risks, but apparently believes that potential funding cuts make this action necessary. PBS President Ervin S. Duggan remarked: "A system driven by advertising inescapably will become a system driven by ratings, and that kind of system can never be driven by the impulse to educate" (Farhi, 1995).

A Commerciality Test for Taxing Unrelated Activities

Charities are human institutions. As such they are in need of some external regulation to correct the tendency to dive to the lowest common denominator of behavior. We are rapidly reaching the point where there are almost no limits on what charities can do to help companies sell products and services. Competition between charities for corporate funding has become so intense that there is a need for an external regulator to establish appropriate standards.

This paper is concerned with the problems associated with the perception of commercial behavior. In this regard, the author believes the Internal Revenue Service may have a point when it tries to distinguish between "active" and "passive" income-producing activities. Traditional "passive" investments—stocks, bonds, even rental property—do require active management by the nonprofit. But, except for real property rentals, these investments generally do not involve the nonprofit directly or indirectly in efforts to market commercial goods and services, nor do they lead to a public perception that the charity is endorsing a particular product or service.

The situation is quite different where the charity is licensing its name and logo to a product manufacturer or service provider. In this situation, the business is bargaining for the charity's implied endorsement to promote sales. There may be instances where the charity really is endorsing the product, as when a charity selectively licenses manufacturers to produce museum-quality reproductions and can establish that considerations of artistic merit and educational value predominate over economic return. However, there also are many instances where the sole selection criterion, subject to some minimal quality check, is which credit card company or long-distance telephone company is offering the best financial deal to the charity.

Charities receiving income from arrangements that help manufacturers sell goods and services generally should be taxed on that income. The sole exception should be where the sale of the product furthers the charity's exempt purpose and is no larger than necessary to fulfill that purpose. The distinction lies between the widespread marketing of ordinary consumer products and sales of specialized goods targeted at narrow audiences that might not be served without the charity's active participation. For example, a charity whose purpose includes assisting individuals with a particular disease or disability might decide to sell a special piece of adaptive equipment for which there would not otherwise be a market. That charity should be able to enter a nontaxable royalty agreement as well as sell the product directly without incurring tax.

Sponsorship issues are related to royalty issues; indeed the line between the two can be rather blurred. The basic issue of sponsorship is how to distinguish legitimate recognition of a corporate donation from a bargained-for advertising opportunity. Some, if not most, corporate sponsors are demanding greater and greater levels of recognition. The last remaining line between sponsorship and all-out advertising lies in the prohibitions in the Internal Revenue Service's proposed sponsorship rules designed to prevent the use of standard advertising language such as statements about quality, price information, and inducements to buy (Internal Revenue Service, 1993). At a minimum it is important to maintain this basic distinction, but the risks of excessive commerciality are such that it is worth reopening the debate, initiated in the Mobil case and the proposed sponsorship audit guidelines, about the circumstances in which sponsorship becomes advertising.

Deciding what the rules should be is difficult. The most likely approach would be one that combines a list of factors, as the IRS audit guidelines did, although the specific factors would be somewhat different. Several questions need to be addressed, including the need to protect smaller organizations that do not have sophisticated tax lawyers and accountants. Another is how to involve the charitable community in working out a set of livable guidelines.

There are dangers in drawing any of these rules too tightly. An important danger is an artifact of the use of the tax code for signaling appropriate behavior. If, for example, placing Mobil's name and logo on a scoreboard becomes a form of taxable advertising rather than recognition of a corporate gift, then there is no further reason for the scoreboard not to contain overt advertising of Mobil products. This result would further the commercialization of nonprofits, not deter it.

Commerciality and Trust

The fascinating debate over the rationale or rationales for tax exemption is beyond the scope of this paper. The author believes that the importance of charities to society lies not just in the services they provide, but in the values they foster and encourage and particularly the values of altruism, pluralism, and community (Independent Sector, 1993).

Altruism is the core value that nonprofits contribute to our society. Altruism is an affirmation that all human beings have a basic moral obligation to look beyond themselves, to undertake activities that contribute to the betterment of other people, other species, future generations. Regard for the cares and concerns of others is a counterpoint to the self-regard that is the basis of capitalism and a foundation for the debate and compromise necessary to democracy.

But if nonprofits are to teach altruism, they must encourage it and embody it in their actions and the public must perceive them as doing so. Commercial practices jeopardize the public's perception of nonprofits as organizations motivated by concern for others, not profit. Bargaining with a soft drink company over an exclusive rights agreement does not foster in that company's leadership any sense of responsibility for the community or the future even if the payment that results is called a "gift." A hospital that survives or fails based on its success in negotiating the best possible deals with third-party payers is not fostering altruism in its community. It is making the best business deal it can.

People still place great trust in nonprofit organizations. No small part of that trust is based on the belief that nonprofit institutions generally will act in trustworthy ways because they are not primarily motivated by the need to make a profit or the need to be reelected to public office. Commercial behavior jeopardizes that trust.

Notes

[1] Terminology is always a problem. This paper uses the term "charitable" in its traditional legal sense to encompass the array of charitable, educational, religious, and scientific organizations exempt under section 501(c)(3) of the Internal Revenue Code and eligible to receive tax deductible contributions. The word "nonprofit" includes the broader array of institutions exempt under section 501(c), but for present purposes effectively adds only section 501(c)(4) social welfare organizations to the mix. Commerciality considerations seem far less relevant for private purpose nonprofits such as trade associations and private clubs.

[2] Within the major subsectors of the independent sector, the percentage of support from charitable contributions ranged from a low of 5.5 percent for health services to a high of 62.5 percent for arts and cultural institutions. Payments ranged from a low of 12.5 percent of total support for arts and cultural institutions to a high of 54.3 percent for educational/research institutions. Data are for 1989 and are reported as preliminary. Payments include both payments from the private sector and government payments (Hodgkinson, 1992, Table 4.3). The table also reports support for religious organizations and foundations.

[3] A recent ad in the *Delaware Nonprofit* (Spring 1995, p. 3) by a professional fundraising consultant made the same point much more directly: "More and more companies are using sponsorship as another advertising medium. The days of a company simply writing a check are ending. Now a company wants a direct return on its investment. Find out how you can maximize this new but increasingly important fundraising tool."

References

Bennett, J. and Rudney, G. "A Commerciality Test to Resolve the Commercial Nonprofit Issue." *Tax Notes*, September 14, 1987, 1095-1098.

Blumenstyk, G. "Georgia Tech and McDonald's Sign $5.5-Million Deal." *The Chronicle of Higher Education*, February 3, 1995, p. A44.

"Business Group Proposes Barring Nonprofits from Competition," *State Tax Trends for Nonprofits*, Summer 1990, 1.

City of Philadelphia. *Report of the Mayor's Special Committee on Payments-in Lieu-of-Taxes (PILOTs) and Services-in-Lieu-of-Taxes (SILOTs)*, June 30, 1994.

City of Washington v. Board of Assessment Appeals, No. 2052 C.D. 1994 (Pa. Commw., September 15, 1995 (Washington & Jefferson College).

"Cotton Bowl Sponsorship Contract Made Public." *Tax Monthly for Exempt Organizations*, May 1992, 3.

Colombo, J. and Hall, M. *The Charitable Tax Exemption*. Boulder: Westview Press, 1995.

Disabled American Veterans v. Commissioner, 94 T.C. 60 (1990), rev'd on other grounds, 942 F.2d 349 (6th Cir. 1991) (DAV II).

Farhi, P. "Now, a Word From Their Underwriter," *The Washington Post*, June 7, 1995, p. A1.

Gaul, G. M. and Borowski, N. A. *Free Ride: The Tax Exempt Economy*. Kansas City: Andrews & McMeel, 1992.

Gray, B. *The Profit Motive and Patient Care: The Changing Accountability of Doctors and Hospitals*. Cambridge: Harvard University Press, 1991.

Grenzebach, M. quoted in *Association Trends*, May 26, 1995, 1.

Hansmann, H. "The Role of Nonprofit Enterprise" *Yale Law Journal*, 1980, 89, 835-901.

Hospital Utilization Project v. Commonwealth, 507 Pa. 1, 487 A.2d 1306 (1985).

Hodgkinson, V. and others. *Nonprofit Almanac 1992 - 1993: Dimensions of the Independent Sector,* San Francisco: Jossey-Bass, 1992.

Independent Sector. *Why Tax Exemption? The Public Service Role of America's Independent Sector.* June 1993.

Internal Revenue Service. Announcement. 92-15, *Internal Revenue Bulletin,* 1992, 5, 51.

Internal Revenue Service. Notice of Proposed Rulemaking. "Taxation of Tax-Exempt Organizations' Income from Corporate Sponsorship," 58 *Federal Register* 5687, January 22, 1993.

Internal Revenue Service. Technical Advice Memorandum No. 9502009, November 10, 1994.

"IRS Relaxes Stance on Corporate Sponsorship." *Tax Monthly for Exempt Organizations,* April 1994, 1.

Leland, P. J. "The Extent of the Challenge to Property Tax Exemption in Pennsylvania: A Survey of 67 Counties." in *Nonprofit Organizations as Public Actors: Rising to New Public Policy Challenges,* 471. Working Papers of the Independent Sector 1995 Spring Research Forum, cited with permission.

St. Margaret Seneca Place v. Board of Property Assessment, Appeals And Review, 640 A.2d 380 (Pa. 1994)

Salamon, L. M. "The Voluntary Sector and the Future of the Welfare State." *Nonprofit and Voluntary Sector Quarterly,* 1989, 18(1), 11-24.

Sheppard L. "Aspirin and the Ultimate Tax Shelter." *Tax Notes,* July 25, 1994, 420-425.

Sierra Club, Inc. v. Commissioner, 65 T.C.M. 2582 (1993).

Sierra Club v. Commissioner, 103 T.C. No. 17 (1994).

Simon, J. G. "The Tax Treatment of Nonprofit Organizations: A Review of Federal and State Policies." In Walter W. Powell (ed.), *The Nonprofit Sector: A Research Handbook.* New Haven: Yale University Press, 1987.

Sound Health Association v. Commissioner, 71 T.C. 158 (1978).

Streckfus and Paul. "Viewpoint: Georgia Tech Takes Corporate Sponsorship to a New Level." *Exempt Organization Tax Review,* 1995, 11, 564-565.

Tax-Exempt Property Steering Committee. *"City of Boston Tax Exempt Property Steering Committee Guidelines."* undated.

United Cancer Council, Inc. v. Commissioner, 100 T.C. No. 11 (1993).

Reorienting the Welfare State: "Bottom-up" vs. "Top-down" Funding

Douglas J. Besharov

When government uses a particular mediating structure to advance its social welfare purposes, it funds specific activities through a grant or contract made directly to that organization. Known as "third-party government," this form of assistance has become a substantial proportion of total government spending for noncash social welfare programs. And the social service arms of many mediating structures have grown accordingly.

Unfortunately, government often selects the wrong mediating structure for the job. And even when it chooses the right one, its assistance often comes with entangling strings that threaten to destroy the very characteristics that make that mediating structure effective. That is why many thoughtful observers decry all government assistance to mediating structures.

Some services, residential care and health care, for example, are too expensive to be funded by the private sector alone, however. If mediating structures are to perform these functions (and many would say that they should not), ways must be found to help them escape what the revised edition of the AEI book *To Empower People* calls "government's fatal embrace." This paper argues that the dangers caused by government funding of mediating structures can be lessened by an approach to funding that is "bottom-up" rather than "top-down." In fact, a bottom-up approach has much broader benefits, and it would be easier to institute than many people imagine.

Do the protections afforded by a bottom-up approach out-weigh the inherent hazards of government support to mediating structures? As we will see, the answer probably depends on the specific situation (especially since government often regulates mediating structures, even when it does not provide financial support). But readers will have to judge for themselves.

Three Axioms

Stuart Butler presents the starting point for this paper's discussion. In *To Empower People,* he writes, "Don't decide—let the people decide for you." Before I describe how this principle might be implemented, it may be helpful to emphasize certain axioms implied by his advice.

1. *Direct government funding of social welfare agencies (including mediating structures) is likely to create the wrong winners and losers.* The process is analogous to establishing an industrial policy; that is, government tries to pick the best service provider (instead of the best manufacturer, for example). Unfortunately, governmental decisions are less likely to be correct than are the cumulative decisions of thousands, or millions, of consumers. Worse, once government funding begins, political pressures make it almost impossible to end support. Thus, in his research on the differences between private and government support for start-up companies, Allan Meltzer found that private decision makers were more successful because they were more likely to abandon an obviously unsuccessful project than was the government. In other words, government is not capable of performing the key aspect of good decision making: creating losers (Meltzer, 1993). Many Head Start providers, for example, were chosen for reasons having little to do with their ability to care for children, and many others continue to be funded even though they are pale reflections of their former selves.

2. *Direct government funding of social welfare agencies can alter the nature of their services and raise their costs.* When government chooses the service (or agency) for clients, it often imposes costly quality standards on the service. Since government tends to impose regu-

latory standards with less regard for whether they result in a better service than do individuals (who must pay for the service out of their own pockets), government-supported services or programs tend to be more expensive than those that individuals purchase themselves. And government often decides that it knows how to provide the service better than the actual provider, so that it often requires even successful providers to alter their programs. No better example of this two-sided dynamic exists than the "quality"/cost differentials between publicly and privately funded child care.

3. *Direct government funding often requires mediating structures to abandon the very features, like religious activities, that make them effective.* Of course, the government, through its police power, always has the authority to regulate the activities of mediating structures even when not giving them money (subject to various but limited constitutional constraints such as the right to the free exercise of religion). But the temptation to attach requirements to the behavior of mediating structures—and the political support for doing so—is greatly increased when there is direct funding. After all, goes the argument, the money is public money and must be spent in accordance with the "public trust."

What I have described as direct government funding can also be seen as top-down funding, an issue widely discussed in the academic literature concerning the "implementation" of social programs (Sabatier, 1986; Palumbo, 1987). In top-down funding, the money is transferred from the government to an agency that, in turn, provides services to its clients. The money usually moves from the federal government to a state government and thence to service providers, but the same three axioms apply to state- and locally-funded programs.

But what if individual clients could make these funding decisions? Although some might select inferior services, on average, clients will do better than government because they are in a better position to determine what they need, and because their individual decisions are less likely to be determined by extraneous factors (such as political favoritism). Thus, the cumulative impact of clients' decisions would likely establish a stronger cadre of services.

Moreover, if individuals rather than government bureaucrats were selecting programs, there would be less chance that institution-distorting strings would be attached. And defense of apparently unsuccessful services or programs would be unnecessary because consumers would simply stop selecting services or programs that weren't effective.

Thus, one way to protect mediating structures is to create mechanisms that transform cumulative consumer demand directly into funding for their activities (that is, without an intervening governmental decision). This paper examines four methods of achieving this sort of bottom-up funding: (1) cash assistance, (2) lower tax rates, (3) vouchers, and (4) reimbursement for copaid services. It then describes the various situations in which one of the other mechanisms seems most appropriate and the residual dangers that they all pose to mediating structures.

Cash Assistance

Cash assistance can be used for those purchases that can be made in the open market with minimum supervision of the consumer. Cash assistance maximizes consumer choice and requires no special regulation of providers. In addition, giving cash allows individuals to spend less than might have been anticipated on the service and to use the difference for other purposes. This approach creates downward pressure on their individual expenditures, on total expenditures, and also on the price of goods and services purchased.

Cash assistance can take the form of a cash grant to specified clients, an automatic tax benefit for designated classes of taxpayers, or an across-the-board tax cut.[1] The best known cash approaches are probably Aid to Families with Dependent Children (AFDC) and the tax exemptions for dependents. The House Republican proposal for an increase in the exemption for dependent children under 18 is an example of using the tax code to provide cash assistance for general purposes.

Food stamps, which are discussed next, are usually considered to be vouchers. However, food stamps are increasingly like cash because there is now a black market for purchasing them. If recipients are willing to accept about a 20 percent discount off their face value, most are able to trade their stamps for cash, thereby escaping the need to spend the benefit only on food stuffs. Moreover, even when used properly as vouchers, food stamps have many attributes of a cash grant: clients are able to use them to purchase any number of different items, so that there is relatively wide consumer choice and corresponding competition among providers.

Recently, welfare agencies have made cash grants available to clients in job training and work programs to pay for child care. Cash grants, as opposed to vouchers to clients or contracts to agencies, allow clients to purchase child care from a variety of informal sources, including family members. Although some advocacy groups feared that parents might seek out inadequate or dangerous placements in order to save money, so far there is no evidence of this.

Lower Tax Rates

Many people would view tax cuts, for low- and middle-income families, at least, as a form of cash assistance. Over the past 30 years, a greater portion of the federal payroll and income taxes has been shifted to low- and middle-income workers and to families with children. One of the main reasons for this shift has been the decline in the relative value of the personal exemption. Eugene Steuerle has provided some of the best analysis of this issue (Steuerle and Juffras, 1991; Steuerle, 1983). That greater tax burden on lower-income workers and families puts added financial stress on them and creates more pressure in two parent households for both parents to work (Besharov and Weicher, 1985).

Some experts justify this shift in tax burden on the basis that low- and middle-income families now receive additional benefits from the federal government. But why do we need to take money from families in order to give it back to them?

Taking money from families (or all taxpayers, for that matter) and giving it back to them in the form of categorical assistance is a way of controlling their spending decisions. So, for example, when tax funds are used to provide student loans to middle class families, we are taking money from one pocket and putting it into another because we do not think that parents can or will save the money themselves.

This kind of forced saving, or intertemporal redistribution of wealth, sometimes makes good policy sense. Some degree of social engineering is probably inevitable. But we do it far more than we should and with harmful results. In fact, the process can easily get out of hand, and can hook Americans on a never ending upward spiral of tax increases to pay for programs designed to relieve the very burdens created by those taxes.

In 1993, for example, the original Clinton proposal to expand the Earned Income Tax Credit (EITC) proposed providing this "low-income" tax benefit to families earning almost $30,000—even as we tax the same families to help pay for the benefit. The administration quickly withdrew this proposal, although I must add that the current EITC has many problems that should be addressed (Steuerle, 1995,1993).

Vouchers

Vouchers force clients to use a specific service or provider (unless, like food stamps, they can be traded for cash or other services). The best examples are probably vouchers for housing and for child care, since they are hard to trade or sell.[2] And since clients cannot pocket the difference between a lower-cost provider and the assumed value of the voucher, they have no incentive to be cost conscious.

Vouchers also increase the tendency of the government to impose standards on the service or program. Generally, to prevent fraud in voucher programs, the government must designate those who may accept the voucher. (Again, food stamps are an exception, because of the large and competitive consumer market for food.) Since the service providers have to be approved, the temptation grows to regulate them—to make sure that the money behind the voucher is not misused.

Contrary to popular impression, tax credits (and, to a lesser extent, tax deductions) are for most purposes more like vouchers than cash—because they can be used only for a designated purpose (if one assumes that the purchases would otherwise not have been made). But what if the purchase would have been made anyway, so that the credit or deduction has no effect on behavior?

Then, tax credits are more accurately considered a cash subsidy to a group of taxpayers who happen to behave in a certain way (or have certain expenditures). Thus, President Clinton's 1995 proposed tax deduction for college or other postsecondary education was at most a voucher and, as some complained, might have been no more than a subsidy to the upper-middle class whose children would likely go to college whether or not the cost were deductible.

An interesting hybrid between cash and voucher systems is "grant diversion." Under this procedure, an individual's cash grant (Supplemental Security Income or AFDC, for instance) is paid directly to someone else: a service provider (such as a residential drug treatment program), an employer (to supplement earnings), or a landlord (when rent goes repeatedly unpaid). Since the diversion is for designated purposes, the payment, although formally denominated in dollars, is more like a voucher. As efforts to reshape the behaviors of public aid recipients grow, we should expect greater use of grant diversion-like mechanisms. A system could be established, for example, that allowed homeless individuals to use their food stamps and any other welfare-like payments to cover their housing and food costs. Christopher Jencks, in his book *The Homeless,* makes a similar suggestion (Jencks, 1994). Requiring a copayment might add additional market considerations to the selection process, as described next.

Reimbursed Copayment Systems

Reimbursement for copaid services rendered requires consumers to pay part of the cost of a particular service, often under a sliding fee scale arrangement. The government then "reimburses" the provider for the rest. Copayments are usually seen as a method of constraining costs or rationing services by making individuals feel the costs of their decisions (or at least feel them partially). Thus, copayment schemes are most attractive when there is a need to encourage recipients to set priorities among what would otherwise be discretionary purchases. Today, they are most often seen in child care programs.

An unappreciated benefit of both total reimbursement systems and copayment systems is that they allow individual choice.[3] Thus, if structured properly, they can provide all the benefits of other bottom-up approaches. For example, even though the government may initially pick allowable providers, it could drop them based on the actual selections of clients: a rule could be established that a minimum number of clients must select that particular service provider over a designated period of time; otherwise, the provider is dropped from the list.

Ordinarily, a reimbursement system, such as Medicaid or Medicare, is subject to runaway costs because recipients have no incentive to economize and providers do not compete on the basis of cost. Copayment requirements help, but program costs are still hard to control. Hence, many programs adopt additional ways to restrain costs, such as by limiting the number of approved service providers (if the number of approved providers is small enough to restrict access). Medicaid uses this approach to limit the number of heart transplants it funds. Income eligibility guidelines can also restrain costs by limiting the number of potential clients.

Conclusion

Except for lower tax rates, each approach described above can be applied to funding any mediating structure, from the family to organized religions. (Because each approach relies on individual decision making, they all would probably survive the challenge that they provide an aid to religion.) And taken together, they provide a menu of approaches that reduce the risk that government assistance will prove to be a fatal embrace for particular mediating structures.

Nevertheless, except for cash, each approach does increase

the risk of greater government control of mediating structures. In fact, this is a real danger even when government does not provide financial support. Government regularly uses its police power to regulate the activities of the mediating structures it does not fund. In many places, for example, church-based day care is regulated even when no public funds are involved.

There is, though, the other lurking problem with government funding of mediating structures: it builds a politically connected constituency for continued (and increased) government spending. In some areas, like education and health care for the poor, such spending is all but inevitable in the modern world; in others, constituency politics can drive up expenditures.

The issue, then, is one of balance. And the trade-offs vary by context. Medicaid and Medicare funding of church-related hospitals, for example, has created client-driven systems without changing the essential character of those institutions (although the issue of mandating abortion services arises regularly).

There may be other funding devices we have not thought of yet. A surge of fresh imagination would certainly be useful.

Notes

[1] For brevity of presentation, I have treated a tax cut as cash assistance, even though it is the taxpayer's own money that is involved.

[2] Hence, deciding to use a voucher scheme requires a prediction of the degree to which they can be sold or traded, and then deciding if the predicted level of abuse is acceptable.

[3] This paper does not endorse total reimbursement schemes, such as Medicaid and Medicare, because while they maximize client choice, they do not provide sufficient incentives for recipients to constrain costs.

References

Besharov, D. J., and Weicher, J. C. "Return the Family to 1954." *Wall Street Journal,* July 8, 1985, Op Ed page.

Jencks, C. *The Homeless.* Cambridge: Harvard University Press, 1994.

Meltzer, A. "Why Governments Make Bad Venture Capitalists." *Wall Street Journal,* May 5, 1993, Op Ed page.

Palumbo, D. "Symposium: Implementation, What We Have Learned and Still Need to Know." *Policy Studies Review Annual,* 1987, 7, 91-102.

Sabatier, P. "Top-Down and Bottom-Up Approach to Implementation Research: A Critical Analysis and Suggested Synthesis." *Journal of Public Policy,* 1986, 6, 21-48.

Steuerle, E. "Is There a Filing Season Foul-up? What's Not Being Said." *Tax Notes,* March 13, 1995, 1709-1710.

Steuerle, E. "The IRS Cannot Control the New Superterranean Economy." *Tax Notes,* June 29, 1993, 1839-1840.

Steuerle, E. and Juffras, J. "A $1,000 Tax Credit for Every Child: A Base of Reform for the Nation's Tax, Welfare, and Health Systems." *Urban Institute Policy Paper,* April 1991.

Steuerle, E. "The Tax Treatment of Households of Different Size." In Rudolph Penner (ed.), Taxing the Family. Washington, DC: AEI Press, 1983.

Nonprofits and the Public Sector: An Evolving Relationship

Peter B. Goldberg

The relationship between government and the nonprofit community has changed substantially in our lifetime. Public perceptions of this changing relationship do not seem to have kept pace with the changing times. Indeed, the seeming lack of connection that the public makes between the government, of which it is increasingly contemptuous, and nonprofit organizations, which by and large still command widespread support, is a potential time bomb for the nonprofit world.

For whatever reason, the American public does not seem to recognize or appreciate the significant dependency that nonprofit organizations have developed on public sector funding. This dependency has grown out of logic and necessity; there were no sinister motivations or Machiavellian subplots that can be reasonably blamed. But now, as we enter a period of looming cutbacks in government funding across many functions, nonprofit organizations suddenly find themselves in very vulnerable positions.

The size and complexity of the nonprofit world—there are now more than 250,000 nonprofit organizations with combined annual expenditures of more than one-third of a trillion dollars—makes generalizations about them very hazardous. Nonetheless, it seems quite clear that the "Our Town" perception of the nature of the nonprofit world is seriously out of date. Nonprofits are not all small, powerless, altruistic servers of the poor, wayward, and downcast who were ignored by government. We can bemoan it or praise it, but it is clear that much has changed in the nonprofit world.

From the turn of the century to the early 1930s, nonprofits were the principle servers of the poor. Many of the mission statements of family service agencies, for example, referred to delivering coal, clothing, and food to poor families. But roles and relationships between government and nonprofits began a significant shift with the "New Deal."

The "New Deal" of the 1930s and the "Great Society" programs of the 1960s led to aggressive government efforts to respond to the needs of the impoverished. Until recently, the bulk of these public sector efforts were provided directly by government agencies themselves. And, while many nonprofit organizations still continued to serve the needs of the poor through a parallel delivery system, government took over the heavy lifting directly. Meanwhile, there began an incredible "blossoming out," in which nonprofit organizations became much more widely engaged in all aspects of American life. Certainly, the nature and identity of the nonprofit community in 1981, when Ronald Reagan came into office, was different from what Lyndon Johnson might have seen 15 years before that, and was vastly different from what Franklin Roosevelt would have seen at the height of the Great Depression.

In its efforts to sharply reduce the size of the "social welfare" budget of the federal government, the Reagan administration latched on to an evolving notion of public-private partnerships. The Reagan administration enthusiastically promoted substantial increases in private sector giving to nonprofit organizations as a way to offset proposed reductions in government funding and the delivery of government operated services.

The notion of a partnership, however, conveys a certain cooperative arrangement between the partners to achieve some desired goal. In that sense, the term "public-private partnership" was probably a misnomer, at least in its early development. To the best of my knowledge, the public and private "partners" never really sat down and negotiated any kind of arrangement which delineated the roles and responsibilities of the partners for the achievement of certain societal goals. (See Notes for a discussion of some successful public-private partnership models.)

The public-private partnerships of the early 1980s were completely resource and revenue driven. Private sector giving did surge. Corporate philanthropy did triple from about two billion dollars a year at the beginning of the decade to six billion dollars per year toward the end of the Reagan era. Nonprofit organizations were the principal beneficiaries of this growth in giving. Indeed, overall giving to nonprofit organizations rose from $49 billion in 1980 to $117 billion by 1990.

But, while private sector giving to nonprofit organizations rose impressively during the 1980s, it also became abundantly clear that private sector giving would still be wholly inadequate to meet societal needs. Moreover, fractional reductions in government spending easily wiped out substantial percentage increases in private contributions. Even after the initial public-private partnership boom of the early 1980s, it was clear to those who were willing to look that government was still the 800-pound gorilla insofar as the funding support for domestic social welfare programs was concerned.

The determination of the Reagan administration notwithstanding, federal expenditures for domestic social programs were not cut too substantially. But the dissatisfaction with government bureaucracies endured and grew. Increasingly, government was seen as an inept deliverer of services. Simultaneously, there seemed to be a growing love affair with the program service delivery capacities of nonprofit organizations. Nonprofit organizations became the darling alternative for those who were fed up with government bureaucracies, symbolically perhaps best exemplified by President Bush's fervent commitment to his "thousand points of light."

Faced with greatly growing needs and demands for their services which clearly outstripped their capacities to respond, one can begin to see why and how nonprofit organizations started down the path of greater government dependency. By the second half of the 1980s, it was becoming clear that the growth rate in private sector giving could not be reasonably sustained and, even if it could, it would still be inadequate. The bigger resource pot was government. And government was becoming more and more enamored with the possibilities of nonprofit organizations delivering services which were once delivered directly by government agencies. One could say that this match wasn't made in heaven; it was made in Washington!

For nonprofit organizations such as those in the human services, the potential of government funding became more and more irresistible. Building public sector funding on top of a secure base of private sector support seemed like a reasonable, responsible way to diversify funding streams and grow good programs. Especially, as private sector giving flattened out, the allure of some public sector support made sense to nonprofit directors, who were justifiably proud of their service delivery capacities.

Government support for nonprofit organizations does not, however, come problem free. Government grants and contracts have more onerous reporting requirements and very strict limitations on how the funding can be used. But, as long as the base of private sector contributions remained solid, nonprofit organizations were able to maintain sufficient, although narrowed, flexibility to fulfill their overall missions.

Family service agencies offer one good example of what the changes in relationship to government funding can mean. In 1970, the United Way and sectarian fund drives provided 61 percent of our member agencies' income. Government funding accounted for 17 percent and fees accounted for only 5 percent. Even in 1980, federated fund drives were still the largest source of member agency income.

Family Service America often advised its member agencies of the risk of being too singularly dependent upon United Way as its future source of funding. There was increasing competition for United Way funds and the dramatic changes in the corporate landscape were already raising concerns about the future stability of United Way.

Funding diversification for family service agencies typically meant securing third-party reimbursements and government grants and contracts. By 1990, the dramatic switch was substantially complete; federated fund drives were providing only 26 percent of member agency income and government accounted for 43 percent. Counseling fees accounted for 15 percent of member agency support in 1990, up substantially from 1985 levels.

For a brief period of time, it appeared that this kind of program mix would provide for a healthy future. But things unraveled quickly. In the post-Aramony period, United Way support for family service agencies is declining. This presents a double bind for family service agencies. First, because United Way support was largely in the form of general operating support, its dollars were the most flexible and valued and could be used to subsidize a multitude of programs. Second, reductions in United Way support have the effect of increasing the dependency of family service agencies on the more narrowed and increasingly restrictive funding from private third-party reimbursement and government grants and contracts.

The cost containment efforts of private third-party reimbursers are well known and have certainly impacted family service agencies. Private third-party payers have the right to squeeze out every nickel of excess cost they can, but it does present serious difficulties for small nonprofit organizations, which have relatively narrow financial margins in any case, and who use any excess revenue over expense not as profit but as a way to subsidize other programs they offer.

The point is that with private giving failing to keep up even with inflation and with third-party payments more restrictive than ever before, we suddenly see this one large and probably representative nonprofit service delivery system more dependent upon government grants and contracts than at any time in its history. In this current funding climate, significant cutbacks in government support could have a crunching effect on family service agencies. Some programs will be discontinued and, in some cases, entire agencies could go out of business.

It can be argued that a certain amount of nonprofit organizational Darwinism is healthy. There may, indeed, be too many small, marginal, and overlapping nonprofit organizations. Perhaps a system shake-up is in order. Perhaps those organizations who survive the funding crunch that looms ahead will be stronger and healthier. Maybe the nonprofit community has become the organizational equivalent of an overpopulated herd of deer that gets thinned out by a long and brutal winter. Maybe a hard-nosed dispassion ought to predominate in this era of presumably scarce resources. I'm not so sure.

The drive to expand the service delivery capacities of non-profit organizations financed through means other than charitable giving has changed the nature of many nonprofits. For better or for worse, many nonprofits have been driven to be more entrepreneurial. In some cases, this has raised hackles in the small business community, which has come to view entrepreneurial nonprofits as business competitors who have an unfair advantage rooted in their tax exemption. For better or for worse, many nonprofits no longer act like nonprofits (or at least the way most of us used to think about nonprofits). For better or for worse, more and more nonprofits are no longer really dependent upon charitable giving for organizational survival. Indeed, other than from a legal point of view, it is getting harder to single out the defining nonprofit characteristics of a growing number of nonprofit organizations.

As we think about both past and future changes in the relationship between government and nonprofits, we have to recognize both the positive and negative aspects these changes bring to the culture of the nonprofit world and to the public's perception of the nonprofit community.

The value of the nonprofit community—to individuals, to communities, and to our national well-being—is enormous, pervasive, and incalculable. The nonprofit community in America is unique and Americans have become dependent upon a healthy nonprofit community in multiple ways on a daily basis. Sure, there are imperfections and a small fraction (but sizable number, nonetheless) of embarrassing episodes of nonprofit behavior and performance. But, by and large, the nonprofit systems in this country are an extraordinary American success story. How do we retain the traditional values and distinguishing characteristics of nonprofit agencies while enabling them to survive in the very different era we are now entering?

We have not really carefully and strategically examined the

growing financial dependency of nonprofits on government financing (or, conversely, the declining financial dependency of many nonprofit organizations on charitable giving). Are nonprofits a better service delivery system than government bureaucracies? If so, why? And, should government funds be directed to nonprofits to deliver services that government used to deliver itself? What happens to traditional nonprofits when they begin to lapse into government dependency? Are they able to retain their traditional values and mission? Does government funding make a nonprofit stronger or weaker? What happens to the value of private contributions? Are we better off with parallel service delivery systems or ones that are frequently intermixed?

The lost opportunity in the forthcoming debate on federal budgets and public sector priorities is that it will once again be completely resource driven. The focus of the debate will be on public cynicism about government and public concern about the federal debt. There will be virtually no discussion about the impact of public sector budgets on the fabric of the nonprofit world, and there will be very little consideration about the value of nonprofit delivery of public funded services. The forthcoming debate on federal budgets and public sector priorities is really a part of a new and epic battle for the hearts and minds of the American public. It is vital that nonprofit organizations actively participate in this great public debate. The insights and experiences of the nonprofit community ought to help shape public perceptions and priorities. The outcome of the debate will certainly impact the future strength and direction of the nonprofit community.

Unfortunately, for a variety of reasons, many of them probably stemming from the passage of the 1969 tax act, many nonprofits have distanced themselves from the world of government relations. Instead of contributing what they have learned, most nonprofits engaged in service delivery have become very passive (although extraordinarily concerned) about the possible outcomes of this great public debate.

Calls to prohibit nonprofit organizations who receive federal funds from "lobbying" Congress seem misguided and selective. While they may not have organizational tax-exempt status, plenty of institutions and individuals receive a great number of tax breaks. Why should major corporations, for example, be allowed such easy congressional access to protect their tax breaks when nonprofit organizations are discouraged from exercising their limited prerogatives to speak out on public policy issues which concern their clients? The barriers which have been constructed to impede nonprofit public policy activities ought to be reviewed to see which ones can be legitimately lowered rather than strengthened. Nonprofit organizations ought to be encouraged to engage in communications, advocacy, and public policy activities to the extent permissible by current law and regulation. The notion that our government officials somehow need special protection from the views and voices of nonprofit agencies does not suggest a healthy partnership in the making.

The advent of the new, "New Federalism," also suggests much stronger roles for state and local governments. The evolution of the relationship between these levels of government and nonprofit organizations also bears watching. Will these relationships tend toward partnerships to achieve common values? Will service delivery streams remain parallel or more frequently merge? How will state and local governments react when nonprofits flex their public policy muscles (though they may not yet have much musculature)? Will resource-hungry municipal governments question the property tax exemptions for nonprofits?

In summary, just like everything else in the world these days, it seems as if the relationship between government and nonprofits is under considerable scrutiny and is subject to rapid change. Nonprofit organizations simply cannot afford to be "the silent partner." It is up to the nonprofit community to assert itself more and to represent its interests and the interests of the clients they serve in the important public policy debates to come. In the school of thought from which I come, I would argue that this is more than an opportunity; it is virtually an imperative.

The nature of the nonprofit world has changed, is still changing, and will continue to change as the future unfolds. These changes carry with them advantages and challenges. The changing relationship to government is part of the changing identity of the nonprofit community. It will be important to understand the forces which have driven these changes and the full implications of change as we articulate and perceive the value of nonprofit organizations in the future.

Notes

One of the very best examples I know of a real public-private partnership is the National Community Development Initiative (NCDI). Started in 1991 by six private foundations and one corporation, NCDI was an ambitious private sector initiative to launch a new generation of community development activities in 20 cities. The NCDI participants packaged $62 million in grants and loans over three years to launch their efforts with an expected leveraging multiple of ten.

When the NCDI funders began to think about a second round of financing, they approached the U.S. Department of Housing and Urban Development (HUD) to participate. As a result of long and deliberate negotiations, HUD opted to participate as a partner—just like the other participants—and committed $25 million in grants to NCDI 2 as part of an overall financing package of $88 million in grants and loans. HUD participates in the governance and management of NCDI just like every other funding partner. While one might argue that, given its resources, the federal government ought to be providing a larger share of the funds, the process of building and administering this public-private partnership stands out as particularly noteworthy.

A second example to consider is the Low Income Housing Tax Credit (LIHTC). Originally passed by Congress in 1986, LIHTC makes tax credits available to private sector investors who provide financing for eligible projects. The goal of LIHTC is clear and the public sector and private sector roles and responsibilities are clearly delineated; the LIHTC has successfully unleashed considerable private sector investments for affordable housing projects that would not have been otherwise available.

Creating Jobs in the Third Sector:
The Alternative to Welfare

Jeremy Rifkin

After years of wishful forecasts and false starts, the new computer and communications technologies are finally making their long anticipated impact on the workplace and the economy, throwing the world community into the grip of a third great Industrial Revolution. Already millions of workers have been permanently eliminated from the economic process, and whole job categories have disappeared, shrunk, or been restructured.

The Information Age has arrived. In the years ahead, new, more sophisticated software technologies are going to bring civilization ever closer to a nearly workerless world. In the agricultural, manufacturing, and service sectors, machines are quickly replacing human labor and promise an economy of near automated production by the mid-decades of the 21st century. The wholesale substitution of machines for workers is going to force every nation to rethink the role of human beings in the social process. Redefining opportunities and responsibilities for millions of people in a society of declining mass employment is likely to be the single most pressing social issue of the coming century.

Social Wages

Until now, the marketplace and government have been

looked to, almost exclusively, for solutions to the growing economic crisis facing the country. In the current debate over corporate downsizing, mass layoffs, and the emerging two-tier society, few pundits have considered the potential role of the third sector in restoring the work life of the country. In recent years, we have become so preoccupied with the market and public sectors that we tend to forget that the nonprofit or volunteer sector has played an equally important role in the making of the nation. Today, with the formal economy less able to provide permanent jobs for the millions of Americans in search of employment and with the government retreating from its traditional role of employer of last resort, the third sector becomes our last best hope for absorbing the millions of displaced workers cast off by corporate and government re-engineering.

The third sector cuts a wide swath through society. Nonprofit activities run the gamut from social services to health care, education and research, the arts, religion, and advocacy. There are currently more than 1,400,000 nonprofit organizations in the United States with total combined assets of more than $500 billion.

The assets of the third sector now equal nearly half the assets of the federal government. A study conducted by Yale economist Gabriel Rudney in the 1980s estimated that the expenditures of America's voluntary organizations exceeded the gross national product of all but seven nations in the world. Although the third sector is half the size of government in total employment and half its size in total earnings, it has been growing twice as fast as both the government and private sector in recent years. The independent sector already contributes more than 6 percent of the GNP and is responsible for 10.5 percent of the total national employment. More people are employed in third sector organizations than work in the construction, electronics, transportation, or textile and apparel industries.

The American people ought to consider making a direct investment in expanded job creation in the third sector or social economy as a means of providing meaningful employment for the increasing number of jobless who find themselves locked out of the new high-tech global marketplace. The state and federal governments could provide a "social wage" as an alternative to welfare payments and benefits for those permanently unemployed Americans willing to be retrained and placed in community building jobs in the third sector. The government could also award grants to nonprofit organizations to help them recruit and train the poor for jobs in their organizations.

Providing a social wage—as an alternative to welfare—for millions of the nation's poor, in return for working in the nonprofit sector, would not only help the recipients but also the communities in which their labor is put to use. Forging a sense of shared commitment to the welfare of others and the interests of the neighborhoods in which they serve is what is so desperately needed if we are to rebuild communities and create the foundation for a caring society. An adequate social wage would allow millions of unemployed Americans, working through thousands of neighborhood organizations, the opportunity to help themselves.

It is often argued that simply providing income or job training is of little help if not accompanied by concrete programs to help educate the young, restore family life, and build a sense of shared confidence in the future. Extending a social wage to millions of needy Americans and providing funds for neighborhood-based organizations to recruit, train, and place people in critical community building tasks that advance these broader social goals, would help create the framework for real change. Public works projects and menial work in the formal economy, even if they were available, would do little in the way of restoring local communities.

In addition to providing a social wage for the nation's poorest citizens, serious consideration should be given to an expanded concept of social income that would include social wages for skilled workers and even management and professional workers whose labor is no longer valued or needed in the marketplace. A viable third sector requires a full range of skills, from minimum entry-level competence to sophisticated managerial experience. By providing a job classification scheme, grading system, and salary scale similar to the ones used in the public sector, third sector organizations could recruit from the broad ranks of the unemployed, staffing their organizations with the proper mix of unskilled,

skilled, and professional labor that would insure success in the communities they serve.

Financing a Social Income

Paying for a social income and for re-education and training programs to prepare men and women for a career of community service would require significant government funds. Some of the money could come from savings brought about by gradually replacing many of the current welfare programs with direct payments to persons performing community-service work. Government funds could also be freed up by discontinuing costly subsidies to corporations that have outgrown their domestic commitments and now operate in countries around the world. The federal government provided transnational corporations with more than $104 billion in subsidies in 1993 in the form of direct payments and tax breaks.

Additional moneys could be raised by cutting unnecessary defense programs. Despite the fact that the Cold War is over, the federal government continues to maintain a bloated defense budget. While Congress has scaled down defense appropriations in recent years, military expenditures are expected to run at about 89 percent of Cold War spending between 1994 and 1998. In a 1992 report, the Congressional Budget Office concluded that defense spending could be cut by a rate of 7 percent a year over a five-year period without compromising the nation's military preparedness or undermining national security.

Perhaps the most equitable and far-reaching approach to raising the needed funds would be to enact a value-added tax (VAT) on all nonessential goods and services. While the VAT is a new and untried idea in the United States, it has been adopted by more than 59 countries, including virtually every major European nation.

The main disadvantage of a value-added tax is its regressive nature. A sales tax falls disproportionately on lower income groups, especially if it is imposed on basic necessities like food, clothing, housing, and medical care. A VAT also places a greater burden on small businesses, which are less able to absorb and pass

on the costs. Many countries have greatly reduced and even eliminated the regressive nature of value-added taxes by exempting
basic necessities and small businesses.

By enacting a value-added tax of between 5 and 7 percent on
all nonessential goods and services, the federal government could
generate billions of dollars of additional revenue—more than
what would be required to finance a social wage and community
service program for those willing to work in the third sector.

Although powerful vested interests are likely to resist the idea
of providing a social wage in return for community service, the
alternative of leaving the problem of long-term technological
unemployment unattended is even more onerous. A growing
underclass of permanently unemployable Americans could lead to
widespread social unrest, increased violence, and the further disintegration of American society.

A Different Kind of Work

In the past, the government has often been accused of throwing large sums of money at the social economy with little of it getting to the people and communities in need. Much of the expense
involved in government programs has been eaten up in the delivery of social services, with little left over to assist the targeted communities. Still, there have been notable exceptions. Volunteers in
Service to America (VISTA), the Student Community Service
Program, the National Senior Service Corps, the Peace Corps, the
National Health Service Corps, and, more recently, AmeriCorps,
are federal work programs established to promote individual service and support volunteer efforts in local communities in the
United States and abroad.

Although the costs of these government-sponsored programs
in community service are small, the economic returns to the community are enormous and often exceed the expenditures by many
times. Dollar for dollar, government investment in work programs
designed to complement and support the volunteer sector have
proven to be among the most cost effective means of providing
social services in local communities. Yet, despite scores of successful experiments and programs in recent years, the money given

over to such programs is small compared with other governmental expenditures in the social economy.

Many traditional Democrats have customarily looked to government sponsored public works programs to hire the unemployed and those who have slipped under the social safety net and into the permanent underclass. More recently, both Democrats and Republicans have championed the establishment of empowerment zones in the nation's inner city ghettos. These designated areas would receive special tax credits and other government benefits to help attract new business. Businesses that employ a resident of the empowerment zone would save up to $3,000 a year in payroll taxes. Despite the political fanfare surrounding the notion of empowering poor inner-city communities, few politicians are sanguine that many new businesses are going to relocate in the urban ghettos of America, or that many new private sector jobs will be generated from the creation of empowerment zones.

The federal government might do better to redirect its efforts away from costly public works projects and quixotic attempts to create model economies inside poor inner city core areas and, instead, greatly expand existing community service programs in impoverished communities. Recruiting, training, and placing millions of unemployed and poverty-stricken Americans in jobs in nonprofit organizations in their own neighborhoods and communities is likely to have a far greater impact, per dollar spent, than more traditional public works-oriented programs and market directed initiatives.

In the debate over how best to divide up the benefits of productivity advances brought on by the new high-tech global economy, each country must ultimately grapple with an elementary question of economic justice. Put simply, does every member of society, even the poorest among us, have a right to participate in and benefit from the productivity gains of the information and communication technology revolutions? If the answer is yes, then some form of compensation will have to be made to the increasing number of unemployed whose labor will no longer be needed in the new high-tech automated world of the 21st century. Since the advances in technology are going to mean fewer and fewer jobs in the market economy, the only effective way to ensure the benefits of increased productivity to those permanently displaced by machinery is to provide some kind of social income. Tying the income to service in the community would aid the growth and development of the social economy and help strengthen neighborhoods across the country.

Restoring hope and rebuilding the social economy ought to become the central theme of a new partnership between the government and volunteer organizations in local communities. Feeding the poor, providing basic health care services, educating the nation's youth, building affordable housing, and preserving the environment top the list of priorities in the years ahead. Providing a social wage to millions of Americans, in return for performing meaningful work in the social economy, will benefit both the market and public sectors by increasing purchasing power and taxable income as well as reducing the crime rate and the cost of maintaining law and order.

Preparing for the decline of mass formal work in the market economy will require bold new public policy initiatives. By empowering the third sector, we can begin to address some of the many structural issues facing a society in transition to a high-tech, automated future.

Notes

[1] This essay is adapted with permission from *The End of Work: The Decline of the Global Labor Force and the Dawn of the Post-Market Era.* (Tarcher/Putnam), 1995.

Empowering the Third Sector: Looking Beyond Government for Solutions

Jeremy Rifkin

The high-tech global economy is moving beyond the mass worker. While entrepreneurial, managerial, professional, and technical elites will be necessary to run the formal economy of the future, fewer and fewer workers will be required to assist in the production of goods and services.

At the same time that the need for human labor is disappearing, the role of government is undergoing a similar diminution. Today, global companies have begun to eclipse and subsume the power of nations. Transnational enterprises have increasingly usurped the traditional role of the state, and now exercise unparalleled control over global resources, labor pools, and markets. The largest global corporations have assets exceeding the GNP of many countries.

While the political role of the nation-state is lessening in importance, so too is its role as employer of last resort. Governments hampered by mounting long-term debt and growing budget deficits are less willing to embark on ambitious public spending and public works programs to create jobs and stimulate purchasing power.

Now that the commercial and public sectors are no longer capable of securing some of the fundamental needs of the people, the public has little choice but to begin looking out for itself, once again, by reestablishing viable communities as a buffer against both the impersonal forces of the global market and increasingly weak and incompetent central governing authorities.

The Other America

The foundation for a strong, community-based third force in American politics already exists. Although much attention in the modern era has been narrowly focused on the private and public sector, there is another sector in American life that has been of historical significance in the making of the nation, and that now offers the distinct possibility of helping to reshape the social contract in the 21st century. The third sector, also known as the independent or volunteer sector, is the realm in which fiduciary arrangements give way to community bonds and where the giving of one's time to others takes the place of artificially imposed market relationships based on selling oneself and one's services to others.

Alexis de Tocqueville, the French statesman and philosopher, was the first to take notice of America's voluntary spirit. After visiting the United States in 1831, he wrote of his impressions of the young country. Tocqueville was awed by the American propensity to enter into voluntary associations—a phenomenon little in evidence in Europe at the time. The French philosopher was convinced that the Americans had discovered a revolutionary new form of cultural expression that would prove essential to the flourishing of the democratic spirit. "Nothing, in my view, more deserves attention than the [voluntary] associations in America," he wrote.

Today, voluntary organizations are serving millions of Americans in every neighborhood and community of the country. Their reach and scope often eclipse both the private and public sectors, touching and affecting the lives of every American, often more profoundly than the forces of the marketplace or the agencies and bureaucracies of government.

The independent sector is the bonding force, the social glue that helps unite the diverse interests of the American people into a cohesive social identity. If there is a single defining characteristic that sums up the unique qualities of being an American, it would be our capacity to join together in voluntary associations to serve one another. The anthropologist Margaret Mead once remarked, "If you look closely you will see that almost anything that really matters to us, anything that embodies our deepest commitment to the way human life should be lived and cared for, depends on some form—often many forms—of volunteerism."

Volunteers assist the elderly and handicapped, the mentally ill, disadvantaged youth, the homeless and indigent. Volunteers renovate dilapidated apartments and build new low income housing. Tens of thousands of Americans volunteer their services in publicly supported hospitals and clinics, taking care of sick patients, including the victims of AIDS. Thousands more serve as foster parents, or as big brothers and sisters for orphaned children. Some provide counseling for runaways and troubled youth. Others are tutors recruited into the campaign to eliminate illiteracy. Americans assist in day care centers and after school programs. They prepare and deliver meals to the poor. A growing number of Americans volunteer in crisis centers, helping rape victims and victims of spouse and child abuse. Thousands volunteer their time staffing public shelters and distributing clothes to the needy. Many Americans are involved in self-help programs like Alcoholics Anonymous, and in drug rehabilitation programs. Millions of Americans volunteer their time to various environmental efforts including recycling activities, conservation programs, anti-pollution campaigns, and animal protection work. Others volunteer their time to work for advocacy organizations that attempt to redress grievances and change public perceptions and laws. Hundreds of thousands of Americans give their time to the arts—participating in local theater groups, choirs, and orchestras. Volunteers often assist municipal government, serving as volunteer firefighters or donating time to crime prevention work and disaster relief. There are currently more than 1,400,000 nonprofit organizations in the United States with total combined assets of more than $500 billion.

The assets of the third sector now equal nearly half the assets of the federal government. A study conducted by Yale economist Gabriel Rudney in the 1980s estimated that the expenditures of America's voluntary organizations exceeded the gross national product of all but seven nations in the world. Although the third sector is half the size of government in total employment and half its size in total earnings, it has been growing twice as fast as both the government and private sector in recent years. The independent sector already contributes more than 6 percent of the GNP and is responsible for 10.5 percent of the total national employment. More people are employed in third sector organizations than work in the construction, electronics, transportation, or textile and apparel industries.

Tax Credits For Volunteer Work

With the marketplace less able to provide job security for millions of Americans, and the government less willing to provide critical public programs to assist families, neighborhoods, and communities, the volunteer sector becomes the last best hope for rekindling the American dream and restoring the life of the country. Nothing could be more important at this juncture in American history than strengthening the role of the third sector. A good place to start might be the granting of a tax credit or deduction for every hour of volunteer time given to a legally certified tax-exempt organization. The backbone of the third sector is still the volunteer. Were it not for the voluntary efforts of tens of millions of Americans, the social needs of American communities would go largely unattended. According to an extensive 1994 Gallup survey, in 1993 more than 89.2 million adult Americans, or 48 percent of the population, gave their time to various causes and organizations in the third sector. The average volunteer gave 4.2 hours of his or her time per week. Collectively, the American people gave more than 19.5 billion hours in volunteering. These hours represent the equivalent economic contribution of nine million full-time employees, and if measured in dollar terms, would be worth $182 billion.

Unfortunately, volunteer time has declined over the past five years, in large part, because working Americans, anxious over diminishing wages and loss of good paying jobs, are spending more hours engaged in part-time work to bring in needed extra income. Unless the third sector is revived, it will become nearly impossible for neighborhood and community organizations to cope with the increasing burden of social services placed on them by a shrinking public sector and diminishing social net.

The granting of a credit or deduction on personal income taxes for volunteer hours given will go a long way toward encouraging millions of Americans to devote a greater share of their leisure time to volunteer efforts in the third sector. While the idea is new, the concept is already firmly established in the laws governing tax-exempt gifts. Certainly, if giving money to charitable efforts is deemed worthy of tax deductions, why not extend the idea to cover credits or deductions for the donation of hours given to the same efforts and causes?

Providing tax credits or deductions for people donating their time to volunteer efforts will insure greater involvement in a range of social issues that need to be addressed. While there will be a loss of taxable revenue at the front end, it will likely be more than compensated for by a diminished need for expensive government programs to cover needs and services best handled by volunteer efforts in the third sector. By extending tax credits or deductions directly to the volunteers donating their services and skills at the point of engagement, the government bypasses much of the expense that goes into financing the layers of bureaucracy that are set up to administer programs in local communities. Then too, improvements in the living conditions and quality of life of millions of disadvantaged Americans inevitably help the economy itself in the form of greater employment opportunities and increased purchasing power, all of which increase the amount of taxable income available to every level of government.

The Politics of Volunteerism

In the 1980s the Republicans rode into the White House, in large part, on the shirttails of the volunteer theme. The Grand Old

Party dominated the political landscape for more than a decade with the plea to "return government to the people." The Reagan forces realized, early on, the potential symbolic and emotional power of third sector images and used them to their advantage, building a Republican mandate in the 1980s.

President Reagan's appeal to homespun values and old-fashioned good works touched a responsive chord. Although the "liberal" establishment was quick to ridicule the president, charging him with being naive, even disingenuous, millions of Americans, many of whom were themselves volunteers and committed to the principles of voluntary association, saw in his message a call to renew the American spirit, and threw their support behind the White House's call to action. President Bush later picked up on the volunteerism theme during his inaugural. In his now famous "Points of Light" speech, the new president reminded the country that the volunteer sector was the spiritual backbone of the American democratic spirit.

Criticism of the Reagan-Bush theme of renewed volunteerism was heard from many quarters. The American left charged that volunteerism was a cynical attempt by Republican administrations to abdicate government responsibility to aid the poor and working people of the country. In the 1980s the volunteer theme became so associated in the public mind with Republican politics that it was, like so many important issues in American life, reduced to a partisan cause. The Democrats and most liberal thinkers and constituent groups either openly opposed the volunteer theme or steadfastly ignored it.

Now, however, a growing number of progressive thinkers are taking a second look at the independent sector. They are beginning to realize that it is the only viable alternative people can turn to now that the market economy's role as employer is shrinking, and the government's role as provider of last resort is diminishing as well.

The Clinton administration has already taken a first tentative step in the direction of creating a new partnership between the public and third sector by announcing on April 12, 1994, the creation of the Non-Profit Liaison Network, to be made up of 25 administration officials who will "work with the nonprofit sector on common goals." The officials will be charged with building cooperative networks between their departments and agencies of government and third sector organizations. In making the announcement, President Clinton said that he had "long advocated the role of the nonprofit sector." He reminded the public that "throughout our history, the nonprofit community has helped our nation adapt to a changing world by strengthening the core values that shape American life." The president said that the Network will create better collaboration between the administration and advocacy and service groups in a mutual effort to solve the problems of crime, housing, health care, and other pressing national needs.

Although the president's action is likely to be viewed more as a symbolic gesture than a change in political paradigms, it suggests both a growing awareness of the potential role of the third sector in American life and the need to create new working relationships between the government and the nonprofit community. The jockeying between conservatives and liberals, Republicans and Democrats, on how best to enhance the profile of the third sector is going to be one of the most closely watched political issues of the coming decade.

Today, with millions of beleaguered Americans attempting to both make ends meet and at the same time continue to volunteer time to worthwhile civic programs and activities, a tax credit or deduction for volunteering time to nonprofit organizations could help make the difference, and could bolster the effectiveness of the third sector as it addresses the many pressing issues facing our communities.

Notes

[1] This essay is adapted with permission from *The End of Work: The Decline of the Global Labor Force and the Dawn of the Post-Market Era.* (Tarcher/Putnam), 1995.

Competing Visions: The Nonprofit Sector in the Twenty-First Century

Nonprofit Sector Research Fund Conference
July 1995
Aspen, Colorado

Conference Participants

Alan J. Abramson, Nonprofit Sector Research Fund, The Aspen Institute

Sue Anschutz-Rodgers, The Anschutz Family Foundation

Karen Arenson, *The New York Times*

Douglas J. Besharov, American Enterprise Institute for Public Policy Research

Nicholas P. Bollman, The James Irvine Foundation

Desmonique Bonet, Nonprofit Sector Research Fund, The Aspen Institute

Elizabeth T. Boris, Nonprofit Sector Research Fund, The Aspen Institute

Mary Ellen S. Capek, National Council for Research on Women

Lori A. Dair, Public Policy Institute of California

Jean Bethke Elshtain, University of Chicago Divinity School

Suzanne Feurt, Charles Stewart Mott Foundation

Janne Gallagher, Harmon, Curran, Gallagher & Spielberg

William A. Galston, Progressive Policy Institute

Margaret Gates, Nonprofit Sector Research Fund, The Aspen Institute

James O. Gibson, The Urban Institute

Peter B. Goldberg, Family Service America, Inc.

Irving B. Harris, The Harris Foundation

Rev. Thomas J. Harvey, Immaculate Conception Church

Tom G. Kessinger, Haverford College

Susan D. Krutt, Nonprofit Sector Research Fund, The Aspen Institute

Valeria Lynch Lee, Z. Smith Reynolds Foundation

Leslie Lenkowsky, The Hudson Institute

Curtis W. Meadows, Jr., The Meadows Foundation

Sara E. Meléndez, INDEPENDENT SECTOR

Michael Miller, ORGANIZE Training Center

Waldemar A. Nielsen, Program for the Advancement of Philanthropy, The Aspen Institute

Julene Pérez-González, Carnegie Corporation of New York

Jeremy Rifkin, Foundation on Economic Trends

Ann Rosewater, US Department of Health and Human Services

Terry Saario, Northwest Area Foundation

Linda Sanders Childears, Young Americans Bank and Education Foundation

William Schambra, The Lynde and Harry Bradley Foundation

Ira M. Schwartz, University of Pennsylvania

Michael Seltzer, The Ford Foundation

Benjamin R. Shute, Jr., Rockefeller Brothers Fund

Hildy J. Simmons, J.P. Morgan & Co., Inc.

Edward Skloot, Surdna Foundation

S. Frederick Starr, The Aspen Institute

Russy D. Sumariwalla, United Way International

Juan Williams, *The Washington Post*

Julian Wolpert, Princeton University

Raul Yzaguirre, National Council of La Raza

DATE DUE

Affiliation

Demco, Inc. 38-293

HIEBERT LIBRARY

3 6877 00217 6435

DATE DUE

Demco, Inc. 38-293